the FORGIVENESS project

of related interest

Shattered Lives
Children Who Live with Courage and Dignity
Camila Batmanghelidjh
ISBN 978 1 84310 434 6 (hardback)
ISBN 978 1 84310 603 6 (paperback)
eISBN 978 1 84642 254 6

Marina Cantacuzino

the FORGIVENESS project

stories for a vengeful age

Forewords by
Archbishop Emeritus Desmond Tutu
and Alexander McCall Smith

Jessica Kingsley *Publishers*
London and Philadelphia

First published in 2015
by Jessica Kingsley Publishers
73 Collier Street
London N1 9BE, UK
and
400 Market Street, Suite 400
Philadelphia, PA 19106, USA

www.jkp.com

Library of Congress Cataloging in Publication Data
Cantacuzino, Marina, 1959-
  The forgiveness project : stories for a vengeful age / Marina Cantacuzino.
    pages cm
  Includes bibliographical references.
  ISBN 978-1-84905-566-6 (alk. paper)
  1. Forgiveness. I. Title.
  BF637.F67.C36 2015
  155.9'2--dc23
                    2014044096

British Library Cataloguing in Publication Data
A CIP catalogue record for this book is available from the British Library

ISBN 978 1 84905 566 6
eISBN 978 1 78450 006 1

Printed and bound in the United States

This book is dedicated to all those people who have shared their story with me over the years and provided the source and inspiration for everything I know about forgiveness.

Foreword

For many years now the work of The Forgiveness Project has shown us that true greatness is found in humility and compassion. The world watched South Africa's Truth and Reconciliation Commission with a sense of awe; when victims and perpetrators of gross human rights violations came forward to describe their experiences and actions it had an impact that we could never have foreseen. In post-conflict situations around the world people saw a different model of conflict resolution. Since then, words such as 'reconciliation' and 'forgiveness' have been taken from their more spiritual contexts to become common currency in secular and political conversation. It was as though the world had come to a dead end in finding solutions to resolve intractable problems and the people who came to the TRC to tell their stories shifted the log jam and created new possibilities.

'The F Word' exhibition that was created by Marina Cantacuzino and opened in London in January 2004 confronts us with images of perpetrators and victims – together. They are deeply moving and shocking as they speak to us of our own brokenness in the face of such magnanimity. The exhibition continues to be seen by many people around the world. It is a powerful contribution to the understanding that all of us, given certain circumstances, are capable of the most ghastly atrocities. It is also a testimony to the fact that all of us have the capacity to rise to a generosity of spirit that can transform the world.

To forgive is not just to be altruistic; in my view it is the best form of self-interest. The process of forgiving does not exclude hatred and anger. These emotions are all part of being human. When I talk of forgiveness I mean the ability to let go of the right to revenge and to slip the chains of rage that bind you to the person who harmed you. When you forgive you are free of the hatred and anger that locks you in a state of victimhood. If you can find it in yourself to forgive, you can move on, and you may even help the perpetrator to become a better person. From the stories that I've heard, read and seen through The Forgiveness Project I have been witness again to the power of forgiveness.

Archbishop Emeritus Desmond Tutu
December 2014

Foreword

This book is one of the most powerful, affecting documents I have ever read. The title tells you what it is about – forgiveness, a familiar and straightforward enough concept for most of us, even if it is an extraordinarily complex issue when one gets close up to it and starts to scrutinize the subtleties involved. Anybody who has ever accepted another's apology – even for some slight offence – has practised forgiveness, but few of us have felt the need to consider the broader implications of this important issue. That is where The Forgiveness Project, Marina Cantacuzino's ground-breaking exploration of forgiveness, comes into its own. This book tells the story of that project, from its early stages of private research and conversations, to its emergence as a growing and increasingly influential movement. It is not a dry historical or philosophical account of the subject – far from it: this is a collection of personal testaments that makes for intensely moving reading. These accounts of how forgiveness has been wrestled with by people caught up in personal trauma and tragedy provide fascinating insights into individual lives and into a central moral challenge that each of those lives has encountered.

My own interest in forgiveness arose in the context of my earlier professional involvement with the criminal law. As a law professor I found myself thinking and writing about issues of responsibility:

In what circumstances are we fully responsible for actions that may harm others? What excuses do we have? What is the purpose of punishment? These are all lively topics in the academic debate surrounding criminal law, and, indeed, in the everyday practice of the criminal law in the courts. I talked about these issues with colleagues and with students but in many of the discussions that I had there seemed to be a vital element lacking. The criminal law may be prepared to excuse in certain circumstances – as where, for example, there has been provocation or coercion – but it is not overly concerned with forgiveness. Indeed, in one view forgiveness may even go so far as to defeat some of the aims of the criminal justice system, given that the criminal law has a deterrent role to play. If you tell potential offenders in advance that they will be forgiven, then the efficacy of whatever sanction you may have up your sleeve is considerably reduced.

That may be so, but it still seemed to me that without forgiveness any notion of a rehabilitative or healing system of justice was incomplete. Forgiveness, it seemed to me, provided resolution that the system otherwise could not achieve. Any discussion of responsibility and its consequences without an element of forgiveness was like a symphony without the final movement. Human affairs require resolution, I think, in much the same way that music does. There is a deep human need for it, just as the ear anticipates and yearns for musical resolution.

My interest in forgiveness in that context led me to explore the considerable philosophical literature that had grown up around the subject in the last few decades of the 20th century. That was a period in which an increasing number of philosophers became interested in debating why we needed forgiveness and in what circumstances forgiving was the right thing to do. It is interesting to observe that this philosophical debate had nothing to do with the religious discussion of forgiveness – indeed it possibly arose precisely because fewer and fewer people were having the duty to forgive drummed into them as part of their religious education.

At the same time that philosophers were debating forgiveness the subject was being aired in a very much more engaged context by politicians and civic leaders seeking to negotiate the settlement of long-running political and military conflicts. This was forgiveness at the macro level – where large groups of people were being urged to forgive other groups with which they had been locked in conflict. Several seemingly intractable disputes were eased in this way through public bodies into whose very existence the principle of forgiveness was written, one of the best-known examples being that of the South African Truth and Reconciliation Commission. These initiatives attracted widespread interest, and many people who might not have thought much about forgiveness suddenly saw its healing power in operation. They also saw an outstanding instance of it in the example of Nelson Mandela, who publicly embraced those who had wronged him. That example had an immense and lasting impact on a world that had grown accustomed to talk of retribution and the humiliation of one's enemies.

I found that my academic interest in forgiveness was to emerge again in my career as a novelist. When I embarked upon the first novel in my Botswana series, *The No 1 Ladies' Detective Agency*, I did not have a very clear idea of the character of the main protagonist, Precious Ramotswe. That, I thought, would emerge as I got to know her better in the course of writing the book. I had not, therefore, planned to make her a particular proponent of forgiveness, but that is exactly what she became; it seemed entirely natural. And so, in the course of the subsequent volumes in the series, we saw Precious Ramotswe often forgive those whose misdeeds she had unmasked. That rather goes against the grain of the classic novel of crime and punishment: the readers of such books very much want the perpetrator to be identified and punished, and indeed feel cheated if that does not happen. Interestingly enough, the fact that Precious Ramotswe always forgave did not attract protest – quite the opposite: the readers approved of her exercise of forgiveness and seemed to concur in her judgement that as long as a suitable attitude of apology was adopted – and sometimes even if it was not – the forgiving of the wrongdoer was still the right thing to do. Resolution once again: if you punish somebody, you are often only punishing yourself. Forgiveness aids healing – lets the healing fountain start, as W.H. Auden put it.

My personal understanding of forgiveness has been vastly increased by reading Marina Cantacuzino's masterly framing of these stories. That sets the scene for what follows – the individual narratives of people whose experiences come so convincingly to life in these pages. Their experiences cover the whole painful range of human mistreatment by others, but what sets them apart from many such accounts is that glowing element of forgiveness. That transforms what might otherwise so easily have been a series of misery-inducing memoirs of suffering into the most extraordinary, positive celebrations of what the human spirit can do to rise above evil – to negate evil not by returning it with further evil, but by stopping it dead in its tracks, by freeing its victims of its hold.

This book, then, has a real transformative power. It is a significant document of the human spirit. It is an important and memorable statement of hope. To read it is like standing in the light of a gentle, healing sun. It is another reason to feel hopeful at a time when people seem to be turning against one another and we are in danger of facing a bleak future of religious and social confrontation. Every one of these accounts is the clearest and most convincing of refutations of those messages of conflict and hatred, the best answer we can give to them. Marina Cantacuzino points out that forgiveness is neither black nor white, but is, she feels, grey. She is right – but what a warming, vivid grey it is.

Alexander McCall Smith
January 2015

Contents

Introduction

'As Mysterious as Love'

In March 2013, towards the end of a talk I gave entitled 'Forgiveness: a Moral Minefield', a man stood up looking visibly disturbed. He admitted that he had been deeply challenged by what I'd had to say and I wondered which of the many victim or perpetrator[1] narratives I'd shared during the past hour had touched him and perhaps resonated with his own unresolved trauma. It turned out, however, that it wasn't these personal stories that had triggered his response but rather my own position on forgiveness. He simply could not understand how someone who had founded and for ten years led a charity called The Forgiveness Project could hold such an ambivalent view of a topic he considered morally unassailable.

For the past ten years I have been confronted by many such assumptions: the assumption that The Forgiveness Project exists to persuade people to forgive; the assumption that it must be a Christian initiative; the assumption that authentic forgiveness is about personal healing and doesn't require anything from the harmer; or conversely the assumption that offering forgiveness without receiving an apology is partial or incomplete forgiveness; and, last but not least, the assumption that anyone working in the field of forgiveness must take a position.

I suppose my position, which may seem elusive to some, is that everyone's response to forgiveness – or their definition of it – is valid because forgiveness is something viewed through a personal lens and every context and all content is therefore dissimilar. Forgiveness as experienced or practised as a means of relieving oneself from the burden of victimhood is intrinsically subjective. As the former IRA activist, Patrick Magee, once told me (referring to the many different personal narratives I'd collected for 'The F Word' exhibition): 'It's clear from reading the stories that forgiveness is a word no one can agree on.' And more recently Canadian-born Amelia Hutchison wrote to me saying: 'The only thing I know for sure about forgiveness is that it looks different all the time.' Amelia was four years old in 1997 when her father was killed in an unprovoked attack having gone to check on a party being held in a neighbour's house.

In this hotly contested territory, the only thing I know for sure is that the act of forgiving is fluid and active and can change from day to day, hour to hour, depending on how you feel when you wake in the morning or what triggers you encounter during the day. Forgiveness may unfold like a mysterious discovery, or it may be a totally conscious decision, something you line yourself up for having exhausted all other options. It may have a strong degree of pardoning attached to it, or it may just be a sense that you have released something poisonous or let go of something heavy that no longer weighs you down. In this sense, forgiveness means not allowing the pain of the past to dictate the path of the future. It requires a broad perspective, namely understanding that life is morally complicated, that people behave in despicable ways and that some things can never be explained.

While experts may pronounce on the multiple meanings and conditions of forgiveness, those who experience it as a healing path know exactly what it means. Yet for me personally, the more I delve into this expansive and complicated topic, the more entangled I seem to become. Not because I am ambivalent about the benefits of forgiveness but because I am reluctant to pin it down. Something that is so multifaceted and has such profound consequences for the human condition should not be consigned to clichés or glib phrases. Whilst frequently invited to speak on the subject of forgiveness, I don't consider myself any real expert. My only expertise comes from collecting people's personal narratives and encouraging and helping them to share these safely. I have become a facilitator, an enabler, a repository of story. I also believe strongly that there is currently a real need to create a place where forgiveness can be unpicked, debated, grappled with and reframed, most especially for those who are uncertain about what it means, who it is for, or indeed whether it is worthy of discussion at all.

One of the reasons I believe The Forgiveness Project has such a strong appeal (often to people who have never thought much about forgiveness before) is that we present the subject in a way that doesn't drive people to forgive. We do not hold forgiveness up as a magic bullet or a panacea for all ills. Rather, the storytellers reveal the journey to be tough but compelling, often painful and costly but also potentially transformative. Rather than claim to have the answers, we invite people to consider some extreme examples of hurt and trauma as a means of examining their own unresolved grievances and thereby enabling them to arrive at their own answers. Our advocacy work is about creating the opportunity for people to choose forgiveness and presenting it as a resilient response to hurt and trauma.

*

I have Tony Blair to thank for propelling me along this path. In February 2003 I went on the 'Stop the War' march in London's Hyde Park where between one and two million people tried to convince our then Prime Minister that invading Iraq was not something that the British people wanted. 'NOT IN OUR NAME!' screamed the placards and yelled the protestors. In the late 1970s and 1980s I had marched in protest against the South African apartheid government, the nuclear arms race and Margaret Thatcher's poll tax – but none of these issues had ever really felt like *my* issue. Now in 2003, with the war in Iraq imminent, I felt a level of frustration and fury that I'd never felt about any political situation before. Common sense told me that the harder you come down on an individual, or group, or country, the more likely people are to reorganize and emerge in a toughened and more resistant way. In other words, no matter how odious Saddam Hussein may have been, I was convinced that attempting to bomb Iraq into a democracy and removing its dictator from power would almost certainly make matters worse. Tony Blair heard the public outcry but he did not listen. The march of one million plus protestors had no impact whatsoever other than to motivate and mobilize people like me. From that moment on I felt compelled to do whatever I could to present the counter-argument more vividly and more forcefully.

My newly formed peace activism probably would have begun and ended in Hyde Park had it not been for two other events which stirred me up and spurred me on. The first was the photograph of a terrified and traumatized 12-year-old boy called Ali Abbas. Ali became a symbol of the random futility of this war after losing both his arms and almost his entire family in a US missile attack on Baghdad in March 2003. I wasn't the only one to be appalled by the haunted look in Ali's eyes as he stared out from the front page of almost every newspaper the day after the attack. Three weeks later a *Guardian* headline from an article by Julian Barnes summed up what many were thinking: 'This war was not worth a child's finger.'[2]

The second thing that encouraged me to do something more than just criticize or complain was when, late one night while watching local London news, I saw a story about a father whose three-year-old daughter had been accidentally killed by a hospital doctor after he had administered the wrong drugs. I watched as the parents, lawyers and hospital staff emerged from the coroner's court and a journalist thrust a microphone under the father's nose, asking how he felt about the doctor responsible for his daughter's death. I expected to hear harsh and bitter words about retribution and litigation, but instead the father said simply that he had crossed the room, hugged the distressed doctor and told him, 'I forgive you.' It was a particularly moving and, at that time, rare moment of television, not least because in the aftermath of the invasion of Iraq this father's merciful and compassionate tone felt distinctly out of sync with the bellicose rhetoric of revenge and payback that had been grabbing all the headlines.

The story of the father forgiving the doctor, and the overpowering sense of impotence and frustration I felt at a war I was sure would only create further bloodshed and fuel yet more violent extremism, meant that I was determined now to start collecting the personal narratives of people whose response to being harmed was not a call for revenge but rather a quest for restoration and healing. I was looking for evidence. I wanted to find examples of parents who had forgiven their child's killer, victims who had met their attacker, former perpetrators of violence who had transformed their aggression into a force for peace. I chose this subject of forgiveness because gentle people attract me more than resolute ones, vulnerability more than strength, and because I have always believed there are very few truly malevolent people in the world out there. I wanted to create a portfolio of stories that displayed people's personal healing journeys, that expressed their power as well as their pain, and most importantly I wanted these stories to be accessible to a wide range of people by revealing the gritty, messy, risky but authentic narratives of forgiveness.

I knew from having been a journalist for 15 years that first-person testimonies often felt more real and relevant to readers than stories interpreted by someone else, wrapped up in analysis or clouded by partiality. I wanted people's own voices to be heard because I have come to believe that hardened attitudes and fixed perspectives can only shift when we hear the stories of others. It seems to me eminently true that: 'A story told at the right time in someone's life can shine a light sufficiently bright to illuminate the way ahead on the map of life.'[3]

The story-collecting phase of this work took place over ten months, was carried out in my spare time, on a scant budget, and with my friend and colleague, photographer Brian Moody. In the course of our journalistic work we travelled to South Africa, Israel, Palestine and America, as well as across the UK, searching for stories that unpacked and wrestled with notions of forgiveness. During these early months I began to understand several key things about this enthralling and contentious subject. I could see how potent it was as a means to healing, but also I could see that forgiveness was a direction rather than a destination, a difficult process in the course of which one day you might forgive and the next day hate all over again. Above all, it clearly meant different things to different people and provoked strong reactions in just about everyone. I decided therefore to call the collection of stories 'The F Word', because in talking to friends, colleagues and strangers I noticed that forgiveness was a concept that cut public opinion down the middle like a guillotine. There were those who thought it was a noble and humbling response to harm and there were those who dismissed it as a useless gesture only serving to magnify the harm done. In short, forgiveness seemed to inspire and affront in equal measure.

I was only able to fulfil my vision and turn the raw interview material into a physical, portable exhibition thanks to the support of two important women in my life: Jilly Forster, who heads the leading public interest communications consultancy Forster Communications and has been a committed supporter from the start; and the late Dame Anita Roddick, founder of The Body Shop and vociferous human rights campaigner. Anita was so moved by the stories I showed her that she offered to sponsor the launch of the first 'The F Word' exhibition. She was intrigued by the complexity of the concept, knowing there were no easy answers for dealing with our wounds. When I asked her to sum up what she thought forgiveness meant, she told me: 'I've never understood how people who experience pain through violence can see any light or any freedom from the obsession of why or how. I've never really believed that I would forgive. But then nor have I ever really understood the cage which anger locks you into. For me, forgiveness is as mysterious as love.'

'The F Word' exhibition became a space of inquiry, a conversation about forgiveness and revenge, a place not to promote forgiveness as the only way to heal past wounds, but rather to explore its limits and possibilities through individual personal experience. The stories reflected the complex, intriguing and deeply personal nature of forgiveness, providing a vehicle for analysis and inspiration rather than dogma or the need to fix. The narratives themselves had no neat ends and some interviewees proved to be resistant to the very term 'forgiveness' despite the fact that their actions seemed driven by an entirely forgiving response.

Rami Elhanan, for instance, a member of the peace organization The Parents Circle – Families Forum, says of the suicide bomber who killed his daughter in a Jerusalem market in 1997: 'I don't forgive and I don't forget…but the suicide bomber was a victim, just like my daughter, grown crazy out of anger and shame.'[4] I've also heard him say many times that the only way to change the endless cycle of violence 'is the ability to listen to the pain of the other'. Everything about this man is about denying the rhetoric of black-and-white thinking and about reducing fear and hate through humanizing 'the enemy'. And yet he is resistant to boxing his experience into one of forgiving.

In the end, while not everyone who features in the exhibition has forgiven, everyone is in no doubt that revenge only fuels further fear and violence. The protagonists have all used their agony as a spur for positive change.

★

In January 2004, with the war in Iraq still a topic of fierce debate, these narratives of hope went on display at the Oxo Gallery on London's South Bank for ten days. The response was both extensive and astonishing. Six thousand people saw the exhibition, we sold out of two thousand printed catalogues within a few days, the media were hungry for the story (coverage reaching 30 million people worldwide) and organizations and individuals all over the globe contacted me to ask if they could use 'The F Word' as a resource for their own peace and conflict resolution work. Many visitors left powerful messages in the feedback book asking, 'What next?' One woman wrote candidly: 'Now I would like to be photographed next to the man who attacked me.' I was overwhelmed; nothing I'd written about in my many years as a journalist had grabbed the public's attention like this. With the insurgency in post-invasion Iraq now already a mounting problem, these stories seemed to tap into an urgent public need for alternative and peaceful responses to violence. I had had no idea that exploring the subject of forgiveness through personal stories would have such an impact, nor that being exposed to other people's healing narratives would stimulate visitors' own personal inquiry. From that moment on, the subject of forgiveness – with all its nuanced, layered, complex, simple and lucent interpretations – would not leave me alone.

The success of the exhibition meant that, later that year, I founded The Forgiveness Project, a UK charity and not-for-profit organization that sets out through storytelling to explore how ideas around forgiveness, reconciliation and conflict resolution can be used to impact positively on people's lives, through the personal testimonies of both victims and perpetrators of crime and violence.

In an era of mounting sectarianism and religious fundamentalism, my main aim was to give people an appetite for tolerance.

★

From the beginning I felt it was essential that the stories were not excessively faith-focused because there seemed a need to free forgiveness from the straitjacket of religion, to make it accessible to people of all faiths as well as those of none. Of course, the Christian perspective of forgiveness, and that of any other religion for that matter, is an important part of the bigger picture, but for too long forgiveness has been unhelpfully linked to ideals of self-abnegation as well as heroic endurance. This means it easily takes on this holy 'other' quality that detracts from the up-down-backwards-forwards-inside-outside-on-off quality it has in reality. I have come to believe that while forgiving has a very real spiritual dimension (because self-reflection and being consciously compassionate are key to the process), it is not necessarily a religious experience. I remember Marian Partington, whose sister Lucy was murdered by serial killers Fred and Rosemary West, telling me that forgiveness was a word that in her mind had become 'barnacled by aeons of piety'.

Not all people of faith, however, cloak the concept of forgiveness with religious meaning. Whilst Desmond Tutu (a founding patron of The Forgiveness Project alongside Anita Roddick) is arguably the world's greatest advocate for forgiveness, the fact that he is a global Church leader never seems to exclude those who do not share his faith. He is somehow able to carry that paradox between the divine and the profane so beautifully, and I know plenty of atheists and agnostics who love the man and admire everything he says and does. This is because rather than adopting a preachy tone he speaks from a place of humility and humanity, injected with sound common sense and often humour too. In a short video he made in 2014 to promote the online Tutu Global Forgiveness Challenge and *The Book of Forgiving*,⁵ co-written by his daughter Mpho Tutu, he dispelled the belief that forgiveness means reconciliation. 'If someone is constantly abusing you, being ready to forgive doesn't mean you have to be a masochist. If you have had someone who repeatedly hurts you, it is far better to release the relationship than to renew it,'⁶ he warns. In other words, if forgiveness is about reconciliation, it doesn't necessarily mean reconciling with the perpetrator; first and foremost it means reconciling with yourself. Making peace with a painful event is what allows people to live with hurt and catastrophe, find resolution and move on.

I am not a fan of the heroic endurance representation of Great Forgivers, and for this reason I tend to avoid the increasingly popular Oscar-style Forgiveness or Redemption award ceremonies which single out a few worthy 'heroes' as winners. How can you measure one person's transformation above another? How can you decide through a competition who is the most forgiving or who is the most reformed? The hierarchy of victimhood is real enough in communities recovering from the divisions of war, and I have no wish to increase this by suggesting that some forgivers are better than others.

If you Google 'forgiveness', or have it as a search feed on Twitter, you will find a nonstop stream of references to it as an over-sentimentalized virtue or metaphysical gift – typically (to quote just one of a multitude of recent such tweets): 'Forgiveness is an amazing, mystical tool that helps us choose God, choose compassion and love.' I respect that these words are meaningful and potent to some people, but equally I know that they are meaningless and alienating to others. The challenge is, how can we change the language and make the act of forgiving meaningful to those who feel they are drowning in a syrupy pool of stagnant dogma?

In 2014, in a *Guardian* article,⁷ the columnist and priest of the Church of England, Giles Fraser, confessed that he was wary of commenting on forgiveness because so much had been written about it in the past 20 years, 'some of it glib, some of it enormously impressive'. He went on to say: '...there is so much sentimentalizing of forgiveness that it blocks out much of our understanding of the real thing. And by sentimentalizing, I mean the idea that forgiveness involves person A coming to have warm and kindly feelings towards person B when person B has done them some enormous harm.' Others have called this forgiveness 'boosterism'[8] or 'forgiveness inflation'. There is something very narrow about this kind of positioning.

Richard Wilson expressed it eloquently when he wrote about his sister, who, in Burundi in 2000, was ambushed and massacred along with 20 fellow bus passengers by Hutu rebels: 'When a profound moral concept is too loosely defined, the danger is that it can come to mean whatever the people who shout loudest want it to. And those on the receiving end of brutal crimes seldom have the loudest voices.'[9] The problem is that the rhetoric of forgiveness may prevent people being held accountable.

In a BBC1 programme *What is the Point in Forgiveness?* broadcast on Good Friday 2011, the then Archbishop of Canterbury, Dr Rowan Williams, warned against forgiving too easily. He told the *Radio Times*: 'I think the 20th century saw such a level of atrocity that it has focused our minds very, very hard on the dangers of forgiving too easily.'[10] The point he went on to make very strongly was that if forgiveness is easy it is as if the suffering doesn't really matter.

My ambivalence towards forgiveness is not in the act, the gift, the virtue (or however you choose to frame it); rather, it rests in how we promote and present it, and how we encourage others to think about it. The conversations we have and the language we use are important so as not to discourage those who see forgiveness as soft, weak or irrelevant, or equally those who feel excluded from this discourse, believing forgiveness to be solely the privilege of the mentally strong or the spiritually enlightened. Proselytizing is dangerous whatever the field, because when a light becomes glaringly bright it ceases to illuminate; instead it just blinds you.

The worst kind of example of this is what I experienced at a public event in London one evening in 2012. A spiritual self-improvement teacher of international repute was in town to deliver a talk to 200 people on the subject of forgiveness. One of the exercises we were asked to do was to group into categories and write down on a single piece of paper everyone we had ever encountered, everything we had ever experienced, every emotion we had ever felt – and then hand in the sheet of paper at the end of the evening for it to be torn up. This would mean that everything from our past could be shredded, forgotten and ritualistically forgiven. As most people were busily scribbling away, one woman at the back seemed frozen by the task and kept putting her hand up in an attempt to get the attention of our teacher. At last she was invited to speak. 'There's one person in my life who does me a lot of damage – must I write this person's name down?' she asked, visibly upset. The point had been made several times that we must refer to *everything* and *everyone*, by group or by time frame, and so it was obvious to most of us that this woman's question was more a cry for help than a need for clarification. The answer came back: 'Yes, write down everything!' I doubted very much whether this forgiveness ceremony based on the ancient Ho'oponopono ritual was going to help this agitated audience member. I disliked the process and quickly gave up writing my list. I noticed a lot of people around me had done the same. I should add here that the Ho'oponopono prayer itself is a wonderful ancient Hawaiian ritual, and its intention 'to set right that which is already right' has a profound purpose in the world today, but this crude variation felt hollow and rigid.

It is precisely this approach to forgiveness that I find depressing – basically the idea that if you can't forgive you will be depleted in some way. It puts an obligation around something that must surely only ever be a choice and which cannot be prescribed or regulated. Forgiveness cannot be deemed right for everyone, no matter how desirable that outcome might be. The speaker at the event that evening made a few claims which made me wince – namely that if you cannot forget then you have not forgiven, or when you get sick it's usually a forgiveness problem as 'you're harbouring some anger in your body'.

The internet is awash with the dangers of not forgiving. I recently read an online blogger proclaim that the advance of Satan was encouraged by unforgiveness. Explaining how it can cause everything from severe depression to physical illnesses such as arthritis and cancer, the blogger described unforgiveness as one of the 'deadliest poisons a person can take spiritually'. While there is considerable research to suggest that having a forgiving nature produces better physical, psychological and spiritual health outcomes, and is therefore an obvious and practical public health tool (Dr Fred Luskin among others has produced some impressive work in this area[11]), to make the kind of generalized statements that link unforgiveness with physical and spiritual disease seems to me irresponsible, creating yet more intimidating dogma. I have become convinced that if you want to encourage people to forgive it is not helpful to bang on about how not forgiving may poison your mind, body and soul.

In 2013, when I was travelling as a Winston Churchill fellow in the United States, I met Dr Mark Umbreit, founding Director of the Center for Restorative Justice and Peacemaking at the University of Minnesota, who, along with Dr Marilyn Armour from the Institute for Restorative Justice and Restorative Dialogue (IRJRD) at the University of Texas, has produced fascinating research on the paradox of forgiveness in bilateral or dyadic settings. The paradox of forgiveness, in, for example, a restorative justice meeting between victim and offender, is that the more you talk about forgiveness or encourage it, the less safe people feel. On the other hand, the more you create the right climate and conditions, the more likely it is that forgiveness will occur. The findings supported what I had already come to understand about the relationship between forgiveness and restorative justice – namely that while forgiveness may indeed be an outcome of restorative justice it should never be an objective. Dr Armour's research has shown that too much emphasis on forgiveness becomes counterproductive. She told me: 'We keep insisting on an explicit concept of forgiveness but that is fraught both religiously and politically. It's too clouded. We need to redefine forgiveness. I'm interested when you see it in the body language, the facial expressions. If you say, "Do you forgive me?" people back off.'

I believe that the non-prescriptive approach The Forgiveness Project takes – of exploring the limits and possibilities of forgiveness through true stories – appeals to those who might otherwise feel excluded from the debate. It is exactly the same with The Forgiveness Project's RESTORE programme for offenders, which comes under the victim empathy and restorative justice umbrella and has been running as a rehabilitation programme in prisons in England and Wales since 2007. Once offenders realize that we are not committed to an ideology, nor are we following a manualized approach to fix them, but rather we are just there to create a safe space to share personal narratives and help them reflect on their own life choices, there is a palpable sense of relief in the room. Hearts open and hardened attitudes start to shift.

I have come to realize that stories told in a therapeutic setting, such as the RESTORE programme, are a soft entry point for people to consider, reflect and decide if they are ready to change. By inviting victims of crime and ex-offenders to come to a prison and share their stories of trauma and forgiveness, we provide opportunities for conversation and dialogue. We are not driving an offender's change. I was encouraged to learn from Dr Mannie Sher, a researcher at the Tavistock Institute of Human Relations and a practising psychoanalytical psychotherapist, that 'people can be so drawn into helping the client/group/organization that they inadvertently take the drive, the desire and motivation from their client. By providing the space and opportunity for dialogue on the other hand, and by being attentive to the story, listening actively and empathically, and only occasionally offering a guiding comment, you can create a wider space for someone to find their own way and derive the satisfaction of having found it themselves.'

This hands-off approach runs through everything that I have tried to create and achieve, but at times it has been tricky. How much easier in some ways would it be to go out into the world certain that everyone must forgive because if they do not their lives will be depleted in some way? But in 2013 I was given good proof that my position can reach people who might otherwise be alienated by the dominating forgiveness discourse. I had been invited to Dubai to take part in the annual BOLDtalks series. In my talk I stated that The Forgiveness Project didn't want to present forgiveness as an imperative within psychology, with sanitized images, moral platitudes or pious-sounding statements. I suggested, as the former Ulster Volunteer Force (UVF) paramilitary from Northern Ireland, Alistair Little, had suggested to me back in 2003, that if people felt compelled or obliged to forgive it could easily re-victimize them.

A few days after my talk a local woman who had been in the audience sent me a message on Facebook to tell me about the breakdown of her marriage. She said that even though her friends and family were saying she must forgive in order to let go and move on, she had come to the conclusion that despite generally being a 'forgiving person' she could neither reconcile nor forgive. At the end of her long message she wrote that my talk had liberated her by giving her permission *not* to forgive. 'I don't wish him bad but I just don't forgive. And I can live with it without feeling obliged to forgive him… Maybe time is a healer. I am sorry that this was a really long msg. But I really felt that you need to know that you did make a difference in at least one person's life – in half an hour!'

★

Sometimes there seems to be a great deal of conviction and certainty in the forgiveness dialogue. I'm uncomfortable with this, mainly because certainty and black-and-white thinking is often just a step away from intolerance, absolute faith, fundamentalism and even radical extremism. As I heard Karen Armstrong, founder of the Charter for Compassion, say in a talk she gave at the Liberal Jewish Synagogue in London's St John's Wood in 2011: 'Behind certainty lies self-righteousness.' Similarly, Brené Brown states in her brilliant 2010 TED Talk: 'We make everything that's uncertain certain. Religion has gone from a belief in faith and mystery to certainty. I'm right, you're wrong.'[12]

Certainty is a comforting, if unsustainable, position to take, representing our burning need for something to hold on to. The Buddhist teacher and author Pema Chödrön identifies this fear of uncertainty as part of the human condition. She has written about how she once stumbled across a *Time Magazine* article on the subject of fear during a long international flight. She recalls that the article 'said that scientific tests have proved that people are more afraid of uncertainty than they are of physical pain. Wow, I thought, that gets right to what I've being saying about the basic queasiness that leads us to all kinds of self-destructive and other-destructive habits.'[13]

I was interested by a recent comment made by Russell Turner who lives in Rancho Cordova in California and whose son was killed in 1995 by a drunk driver. Russell has twice met the man who killed his son through a restorative justice process in prison. Russell's comment (2014) came in response to a question posed by a member of the online Facebook group Restorative Justice

International.[14] The questioner had asked: 'Is remorse essential to restorative justice?' In other words, should victims only meet their offenders if genuine remorse had been shown? Most people would answer this question with a 'yes', but Russell's response was refreshing. 'Essential is an interesting choice of word,' he wrote. 'I find we often look for a definitive answer to elements that make up restorative justice. My victim journey and others I have learned are so diverse, it seems hard to pin down. When we try to define the act of seeking Justice and loving Mercy it is always messy. I know my journey has seen forgiveness, remorse, anger, peace, answers, frustration and hope. We all want certainty, and often what we need is grace on the journey.'

Whilst I am as capable of moral indignation as anyone else, I have for a long time been drawn to Rumi's unconditional field of love. The 13th-century Persian poet, mystic and scholar wrote: 'Out beyond ideas of right doing and wrong doing, there is a field. I'll meet you there.'[15]

This is really why I created The Forgiveness Project, as a place of inquiry and conversation – not as a place to set out fixed processes, or pronounce on the meaning and definition of forgiveness. 'To be conscious that you are ignorant is a great step to knowledge,' wrote Benjamin Disraeli in his 1845 novel *Sybil*. I am tempted by the freeing position of simply not knowing. In *Letters to a Young Poet*, the German poet Rainer Maria Rilke wrote:

I beg you, as much as I can, dear sir, to be patient toward all that is unsolved in your heart and to try to love the *questions themselves* like locked rooms and like books that are written in a very foreign tongue. Do not seek the answers, which cannot be given you because you would not be able to live them. And the point is, to live everything. *Live* the questions now. Perhaps you will then gradually, without noticing it, live along some distant day into the answer.[16]

Cathy Harrington, the mother of a murdered child, reminded me of this when she said: 'Lots of things in life are senseless. There's so much we can't explain, but we need to be able to love the questions.' Cathy said this at the end of a long interview with me on a warm October day in 2013, exactly, nine years to the day since her 26-year-old daughter was murdered. Leslie was stabbed to death in a house she was sharing with two other young women in the Napa Valley, one of whom was also killed. I was in New York at the time of the interview and Cathy had flown from Michigan especially to meet me in order to bring something positive to an anniversary of such pain.

Khaled al-Berry articulated the reason why I am so reluctant to nail things down and fix them. As a former member of the radical Islamist Egyptian group al-Gama'a al-Islamiya, Khaled eventually moved away from the movement, coming to an important realization that 'the most dangerous thing in life is to let people become convinced that truth has just one face'. His memoir *Life is More Beautiful than Paradise*[17] provides a rare and valuable insight into how easily the young idealist can become radicalized by sects who believe that their truth is absolute. In a similar vein, some years previously I attended a discussion at the Tricycle Theatre in London which involved two doctors – an Israeli and a Palestinian. During the conversation the Israeli doctor appealed to his country's leaders, warning that the most precarious thing for peace was believing you had all the answers. His comments made a deep impression on me and continue to do so because we live in a time where absolute and hard-line views seek to categorize, change or eliminate those who are different from us.

If forgiveness was a colour, for me it would be grey, the colour of compromise and conciliation, and because it sits between the two extremes of black and white. Apparently, the human eye can distinguish not 50 but 500 shades of grey, and fittingly the artist Odilon Redon called it the 'soul of all colour'. In the documentary film *Beyond Right and Wrong*,[18] which features the forgiveness stories of several people I'm well acquainted with, one scene particularly moves me. It is when Robi Damelin talks about the moment in 2002 when her son David, aged 27 and studying for a Masters in Philosophy of Education, was called up as a reserve soldier in the Israeli army. Robi describes how David was deeply conflicted about whether or not to go, but in the end he decided to. She acknowledges he was following orders, but more than that he was hoping to be a soldier with humanity. It was a decision that cost him his life, as the following day he was shot dead by a Palestinian sniper. 'The problem is we look at the world as black and white, nobody sees the grey,' says Robi, 'nobody understands this kid who belonged to the peace movement and who was torn about where his duties lay.' More recently, in July 2014, as the conflict in Gaza between Israelis and Palestinians began to escalate again, Robi wrote this poignant plea in an article for *The Huffington Post*: 'How I wish I could view life through certain eyes of black and white and that the grey picture which keeps on creeping in would not shake up my opinions to let me know that I do not have the monopoly on truth.'[19]

★

There is no doubt that forgiveness can cause friction. Victims who have chosen to forgive have told me of instances where family members have distanced themselves, believing it to be an act of betrayal. Shad Ali, who was a victim of a brutal attack in Nottingham, England, had to prevent his friends from taking revenge. He explains: 'I received a huge amount of criticism and confusion from friends and family who didn't understand why I wanted to forgive – especially from my wife who initially felt nothing but hatred towards this man.'

Forgiveness can affront people. Many people see it as betrayal, soft on justice, condoning the offence and letting the perpetrator off the hook. Members of The Association of Jewish Refugees took issue with the rabbi of a Liberal Jewish Synagogue in London in January 2005 for showing 'The F Word' exhibition to mark Holocaust Day. Their objection was, how can a synagogue host an exhibition with a title that implies the promotion of forgiveness during a week which commemorates genocide? A little while later, when 'The F Word' was displayed in the North of England, one personal response written in the comment book was from a father of a murdered Special PC in Northern Ireland: 'It is easy to write in this book and express moving, humbling, inspiring sentiments. It is not easy to forgive and forget. Our son was taken from us by the evil IRA. We shall have a permanent loathing for his killers. No compassion, no forgiveness. Never.'

Also, in certain quarters of South Africa, people were disgusted with me for sullying the sacred word of forgiveness by associating it through the name of the exhibition with a 'cheap and offensive' four-letter swear word.

Some people have every right to feel angry that an organization gives a voice to those who once used violence. In 2009, on the 25th anniversary of the Brighton bombing, which killed five people during the Conservative Party Conference, The Forgiveness Project held an event in collaboration with the All-Party Parliamentary Group on Conflict Issues at the House of Commons. What made this event newsworthy was that the keynote speakers were Jo Berry, whose father had been killed by the bomb, and Patrick Magee, the former IRA activist who had been responsible for planting it. I was acutely aware that Patrick's presence in Parliament was likely to offend some people, and so I wrote in advance to all three leaders of the main political parties to inform them, as well as to those who had been most directly affected by the bomb, namely Lord Tebbit and Lord Wakeham. I wrote as a matter of courtesy, saying that I knew having the Brighton bomber speak in the House of

Commons would bring up difficult feelings, and I explained that The Forgiveness Project was an organization that explored (rather than propagated) forgiveness through the personal stories of real people. I stressed, in particular to Norman Tebbit, who had been badly injured in the blast and whose wife was left paralyzed and in a wheelchair, that his belief that repentance was a condition of forgiveness was as valid as the views of any other victim. Not believing Patrick Magee to have sufficiently repented, this was for Lord Tebbit non-negotiable. I received a frank and fierce letter back, concluding with the sentence: 'Your project excuses, rewards, and encourages murder.'

What I would say in response to Lord Tebbit, and to all those who agree with him, is that certainly these perpetrator narratives humanize violence but only in so much as they expose the pain, the hurt and the legacy. I do not 'excuse' murder. I seek to understand and explain, but never to justify or condone. For victims there is often a strong need to face the enemy; seeing the human face makes that person seem less of an 'evil monster' and the world therefore a less terrifying place. There's an expression 'the poison and the antidote are brewed in the same vat' and that's why I strongly believe that the way to prevent young people being enticed into violent extremism is to hear the stories of those who have been there before. This is why The Forgiveness Project uses ex-offenders to deliver its prison programme, and this is why former perpetrator narratives are placed in this book side by side with victim/survivor narratives.

I understand that Lord Tebbit feels aggrieved that he has never received an apology for the hurt done to him and his family. Certainly forgiveness is much easier if remorse is shown and apology offered, and for some people both are a condition of forgiveness. But I am reminded of a BBC Radio 4 *Today* programme that I heard some time in 2009 featuring the late Reverend Ian Paisley. When asked in the interview how he could possibly sit in parliament alongside his long-time enemy, Martin McGuinness, his response was simple: he said that repentance should be measured by how you live your life now.

★

Everything I've learnt about this thorny subject of forgiveness has come from the people who have generously shared their stories with me from 2003 to the present day. These 130-plus stories now feature on The Forgiveness Project website, attracting 500 visitors a day from all corners of the world.

Father Michael Lapsley, who in 1990 lost both hands in a letter bomb sent by the security forces of the apartheid government, helped me to understand that some people reasonably require reparation before forgiveness is possible. At the same time he also suggested that, in terms of healing for the victim, often apology and acknowledgement are more powerful and more effective than punishment. And, in London, in front of a gripped audience, Father Michael once argued that forgiveness could be seen as an act of aggression. What he meant was that if you tell someone you forgive them when they don't think they've done you any harm, they may quite understandably become angry and defensive.

When I first began collecting these forgiveness stories, Alistair Little, the former Ulster Volunteer Force (UVF) paramilitary turned peacebuilder from Belfast, instilled in me a real reluctance to sanitize the subject and helped me to understand that to expect victims and survivors to forgive was to lay a further tyranny on them. Of his own offence of killing a man in 1975 during Northern Ireland's bitter sectarian fighting, he said: 'I don't think I have a right to ask for forgiveness. It only adds insult to injury and places yet another burden upon relatives and family members.'[20]

Jo Berry articulated beautifully an integral component of forgiveness: empathy – the ability to stand in someone else's shoes, no matter how dirty or ill-fitting they may be. She told me how she was finally able to reach a point where she could say about the man responsible for her father's murder in the Brighton bombing: 'If I had lived your life, perhaps I would have made your choices.'

Arno Michaelis helped me to realize that it was somehow limiting when people said genuine forgiveness had to be earned and deserved. He showed me that unconditional forgiveness from victims could in fact rehabilitate the offender. Once a white supremacist responsible for countless acts of violence, Arno was still full of hate when some of those he reviled showed him compassion. Now he believes: 'Forgiveness is a sublime example of humanity that I explore at every opportunity, because it was the unconditional forgiveness I was given by people whom I once claimed to hate that demonstrated for me the way from there to here.'

Judith Toy, who lost several members of her family in a brutal and unprovoked attack in America, taught me that forgiveness requires forbearance and may never lead to reconciliation. Talking about a very different family matter, she said: 'I have a brother who doesn't speak to me... I have reached out to him many times, but he is intractable. Reconciliation does not always flow, but I have learned to be patient.'

Cathy Harrington spoke about something many other devastated and traumatized victims have hinted at, but which I'd never fully understood before meeting her in New York. She spoke about this sense that recovery is about transforming the trauma into something which has meaning. This doesn't mean making sense of it (vicious crimes are senseless and inexplicable after all), but rather it is what the American academic Dr Marilyn Armour has called *meaning-making*, the 'intense pursuit of what matters'. In the case of Cathy, whose daughter was murdered in an appalling act of brutality, she has directed her life towards what she describes as 'writing Leslie's gospel' – in other words, creating a legacy for her daughter. This then becomes the 'intense pursuit of what matters'. The healing process is to pass from the narration of an offence as hurt feelings into a narration of the offence as an experience of significance.

Letlapa Mphahlele summed up for me why an eye for an eye simply cannot work. Letlapa was the former Director of Operations of the military wing of the South African Pan Africanist Congress (PAC) during the apartheid era. His justification for using violence in the struggle against apartheid started to shift when many years later he met the mother of one of his victims, Ginn Fourie. He explains: 'I believed that terror had to be answered with terror, and I authorized high-profile massacres on white civilians in the same way that our oppressors had done to us. At the time it seemed the only valid response. But where would it have ended? If my enemies had been cannibals, would I have eaten white flesh? If my enemies had raped black women, would I have raped white women?'

Renny Cushing, who in 2004 founded Murder Victims' Families for Human Rights (www.mvfhr.org) in America, and whose father was murdered in the family home in 1988, has responded eloquently to the question of how people who have lost a family member to murder can possibly be opposed to the death penalty. He argues: 'Not only would my father have been taken from me, but so too would my values... I think it is the same for all of us as a society... If we let those who kill turn us into killers and evoke violence and evil from us, we are much the worse for it.'[21] In other words, the desire to mete out equal injury to those who have harmed others means we may become a little like them ourselves. The popular notion that retribution helps the victim may therefore be a delusion.

Renny Cushing has also told me he is wary of creating or reinforcing a hierarchy of victims or an implicit assumption that some actions of victims make them morally superior to other victims:

In my experience the death penalty abolition movement tends to celebrate victims like myself who oppose the death penalty, and scorn and denigrate victims who support capital punishment. Abolitionists celebrate victims who 'forgive' but judge those people who don't forgive as lesser, perhaps immoral. I really don't like that. It makes me separate from people with whom I have so much in common – the unmentionable pain of closing a casket on the bullet-riddled body of a loved one – and I prefer solidarity in journeys toward healing in the aftermath of homicide.

★

I have come to believe that it is unhelpful to talk of forgiveness when people are right in the middle of battle, whether that battle is with malicious siblings or massacring tribes. Some few individuals will be able to line themselves up to forgive right from the point of crisis, perhaps spurred on by a deep religious or moral conviction, but most of us will not be ready. In the middle of battle all we can do is concentrate on survival, on getting through and protecting our own. Whether victim or perpetrator, there is no time for reflection; and forgiveness, whether for self or for other, requires reflection. In my mind, forgiveness becomes tangible and useful when it is part of a renewal process; when it involves repairing damaged relationships or rebuilding fractured communities; when it can heal grievances that extend and fester across generations. This is because the act of forgiving can turn a page, write a new chapter.

In Marian Partington's remarkable memoir *If You Sit Very Still*, depicting her own healing journey following her sister's murder, she eloquently explains how forgiveness could only surface after a whole sequence of emotional responses to trauma that began with the simple act of having compassion for her own pain.

Remembering standing by Lucy's grave with the 'demolition of my sister and the suffering that followed in its wake, spreading its pain with the indifference and terrible destruction of an earthquake', her mind is filled with anger and contempt. She therefore concludes:

> This business of forgiveness must go on hold. It almost seemed obscene: to think about forgiveness would be a betrayal of our need to grieve, to rage, to find a way forward. It was necessary to dissolve my own grief and anger and find compassion for myself before opening myself to the possibility of forgiving those who caused this terrible pain.[22]

One of the reasons forgiveness is so tricky is that some wrongdoers seem so entirely undeserving of it. The list of high-profile murderers, sadists and tyrants is endless, but, to name just a few, how on earth do you start to forgive the likes of Hitler, Pol Pot, Kim Il Sung, or Abubakar Shekau, the leader of Nigeria's Islamist group Boko Haram who in 2014 abducted over 200 schoolgirls just for receiving a Western education? How do we talk of forgiveness in relation to these grand-scale atrocities where the human capacity for evil seems limitless? It is probably not our place to grant forgiveness when we have not been directly harmed ourselves, but for those who have I think forgiveness looks something like what Marian Partington describes in her deliberations around forgiving Rosemary West for the murder of her sister: 'Her story seems to be about the impoverishment of a soul that knew no other way to live than through terrible cruelty.' For Marian, forgiveness begins with a commitment to recognize Rosemary West's humanity as well as a refusal to demonize her.

In this sense, forgiveness is not about excusing people but about embracing human frailty and fallibility and taking responsibility for a society we may have helped to create. Andrea LeBlanc, whose husband was killed when the second plane was flown into the World Trade Center in 2001, and who is a founding member of

September Eleventh Families for Peaceful Tomorrows, has tried to reframe our thinking about evil acts by suggesting that each one of us may have a part to play. Responding to the savage shootings of 20 young children and six adults in Sandy Hook Elementary School in Connecticut in 2012, Andrea wrote: 'There are no words that will assuage the victims' families' grief...the wounds will remain.' But she said: 'We need to understand that the gunman and his family are victims too. Perhaps victims of the society we have responsibility for.'[23]

When Phyllis Rodriguez,[24] whose son was killed when the Twin Towers were attacked in 2001, was asked on a radio programme how she felt towards Zacarias Moussaoui who had recently been charged with conspiracy in connection with the atrocity, she said: 'If empathy means seeing him as a fallible human being who's capable of evil *and* capable of good – yes, then sure I have empathy for this man, because I believe under the right circumstances I'm also capable of evil.'

Samantha Lawler, a young woman from Florida whom I first met in 2013, summarized something for me that I'd also observed over my many years of story collecting: namely that those who forgive seem to possess a broader, more flexible perspective of human ethics than those who do not. Talking about forgiving her father for the murder of her mother, she puts it like this: 'Forgiveness is not about forgiving the act but forgiving the imperfections which are inherent in all of us.' Her statement demonstrates that forgiveness is more than acceptance and letting go because it requires a degree, even if the very smallest degree, of empathy or compassion. Stephen Cherry quotes the pastoral theologian John Patton in his book *Healing Agony: Re-imagining Forgiveness*: 'Forgiveness is not something that is done but something that is discovered.' The relevant discovery, as far as Patton is concerned, is that the offender is 'human like myself'.[25] My collaborator on a website resource analyzing many of The Forgiveness Project stories – www.theforgivenesstoolbox.com – has put it even more concisely. Speaking at a conference on collective victimology in Verona in 2014, Dr Masi Noor, a senior lecturer in psychology, concluded: 'Forgiveness isn't a pro-social act born out of the victim's generosity but a rehumanizing gift emphasizing the humanity of the perpetrator.'

So when people forgive appalling acts of cruelty, it is not the offence they forgive but humanity itself for failing. They empathize not because they tolerate the wrongdoing but because they have compassion for people with twisted minds hell-bent on cruelty, what Shakespeare describes as 'ruined pieces of nature'.[26] And somehow they are able to stand in these dirty shoes and imagine something of what it is like to be born with such aberrant compulsions. Certainly justice means that once caught and convicted these perpetrators of evil acts must be locked away – but many will ask, are they deserving of compassion too? Can these so-called 'animals' and 'monsters' ever be candidates for redemption? I would argue that if they are simply a manifestation of an external evil force separate from the rest of us, then the answer has to be no. But perhaps evil in this sense means that something has gone badly wrong, that they have been brutally brainwashed or their mind has been wired defectively (whether a fault at birth or a trauma in childhood), giving such individuals a limited capacity for remorse, little emotional awareness and no ability to distinguish right from wrong. Remorse in this sense is simply a muscle that has never been exercised and therefore has no function or power. Empathy doesn't mean feeling sorry for someone or having pity; it simply means having the ability to put yourself in someone else's shoes, no matter how soiled and sordid those shoes may be.

Marian Partington indicated some of this to me once when referring to the restorative work she had done with lifers and other dangerous prisoners. Referring to the pit of despair she felt after discovering the brutal way her sister had been killed, she confessed she had felt 'a connection with all those who are tortured by the imprisoning hell of their own minds'. This embraces the South African concept of *ubuntu*, the radical realization that my humanity is inextricably caught up in yours, a concept Desmond Tutu described at The Forgiveness Project's annual lecture in 2010 as 'the essence of being human... I am me because you are you.' The author David Mitchell puts it another way in his powerful and intense novel *Cloud Atlas*: 'Our lives are not our own. From womb to tomb, we are bound to others. Past and present. And by each crime and every kindness, we birth our future.'[27]

I profoundly agree with the words of Aleksandr Solzhenitsyn from *The Gulag Archipelago 1918–1956* in which the Russian writer and dissident gives a striking explanation of why we prefer not to take responsibility for humanity's most heinous crimes:

> If only there were evil people somewhere insidiously committing evil deeds, and it were necessary only to separate them from the rest of us and destroy them. But the line dividing good and evil cuts through the heart of every human being. And who is willing to destroy a piece of his own heart?[28]

When I discovered this quote a year into collecting the forgiveness stories, I realized that this was the essence of the ethos that lay at the heart of my work. Later in the book, Solzhenitsyn explains more fully what he means:

> Gradually it was disclosed to me that the line separating good and evil passes not through states, nor between classes, nor between political parties either, but right through every human heart, and through all human hearts. This line shifts. Inside us, it oscillates with the years. Even within hearts overwhelmed by evil, one small bridgehead of good is retained; and even in the best of all hearts, there remains a small corner of evil. (p.312)

A few years ago my aunt translated the letters of her father and my Romanian grandfather, George Matei Cantacuzino, who died aged 61 in Romania and whom I never knew. Following the Communist occupation of his country in 1944 and 'incapable of dancing to the Marxist tune' (as he wrote in one letter), he was later arrested trying to escape and sentenced to forced labour at the Danube–Black Sea Canal, amounting to five years' imprisonment from 1948 to 1953. In the final years of his life he took refuge in letter-writing – letters contemplating love, nature, memory and the proximity of good and evil. Many of these letters were written to his English friend, Simon Bayer, whom he had met whilst fighting in the First World War. One letter in particular, written in 1955, caught my attention. In it my grandfather ponders the effect of his five years as a political prisoner, addressing his correspondent's presumption that his past ordeals must surely mean he is filled with bitterness. He writes: 'I think of evil as inherent in human nature, as the natural shadow cast by good. I do not have any feelings of resentment. Because I do not stand in judgement on the actions of others, I have nothing to forgive.'[29]

I find it hard to imagine forgiving anyone who might do terrible harm to my family and children. However, having met so many people who have managed to take this path and create a life beyond their suffering, I know it is the space I would prefer to occupy. I have seen how the act of forgiving unsticks you from the trauma and awakens new possibilities and hopes. Forgiveness, as Marian Partington has described, is 'a creative response', or, in words attributed to author Mark Twain, 'the fragrance that the violet sheds on the heel that has crushed it'.

The words of Philip Zimbardo in his seminal book *The Lucifer Effect*[30] make perfect sense to me. Theorizing on how good people turn evil, he writes: 'With public fear notched up and the enemy threat imminent, reasonable people act irrationally, independent people act in mindless conformity, and peaceful people act as warriors' (p.11). According to the late Alison Des Forges, a human rights activist and historian who tried to call the world's attention to the impending genocide in Rwanda, such behaviour lies just under the surface of any of us. Zimbardo quotes Des Forges as having said: 'The simplified accounts of genocide allow distance between us and the perpetrators of genocide. They are so evil we couldn't ever see ourselves doing the same thing' (p.15). Des Forges knew from investigating many atrocities that minds can be so efficiently brainwashed that formerly peace-loving citizens are persuaded to massacre their neighbours and support an ideology that purports punishing the powerful by murdering the innocent. We fear that if we engage with evil people we might discover they are human just like us, but we also fear we will reduce and lower our own morality to the same level as them. I am reminded of the German philosopher Friedrich Nietzsche, when he warned in *Beyond Good and Evil*: 'He who fights with monsters should be careful lest he thereby become a monster.'[31]

*

In Pumla Gobodo-Madikizela's *A Human Being Died That Night*,[32] the psychologist reports and reflects on her interviews with the commanding officer of state-sanctioned death squads under the South African apartheid regime, Eugene de Kock. She writes: 'If memory is kept alive in order to cultivate old hatreds and resentments, it is likely to culminate in vengeance, and in a repetition of violence. But if memory is kept alive in order to transcend hateful emotions, then remembering can be healing' (p.103).

I have found that part of reparation for both victims and offenders is being able to share their story with others. My intention has always been to present healing narratives and facilitate restorative storytelling in the hope that it will allow people to reconcile with trauma, offer hope for a better future and explore peaceful solutions to violence. The stories not only represent a model for repairing broken communities or releasing toxic relationships but also shed light on our own smaller grievances by building empathy and providing fresh perspectives on difficult situations. A fellow peace activist once told me that during a visit to Northern Ireland in 2000 the Dalai Lama urged a victim of the violence to 'get up' and use her story to 'help others'. The woman, who had been unable to leave her home since her husband's assassination some years previously, had indeed taken this strict but compassionate advice and was much the better for it.

So many of the people whose stories I've helped to tell over the years seem motivated by what I think is best summed up by Assaad Chaftari. Assaad was a former intelligence official in the Christian militia during the Lebanese Civil War and therefore responsible for many deaths over many years. When I asked him about his steady transformation away from violence and the consequences of his open letter to the Lebanese people asking for their forgiveness (published in the Lebanese press in 2000), he articulated what I am sure so many other storytellers must also have felt. He said: 'I've given my life over to working for peace, even if it means sometimes making great sacrifices. I would venture into the jaws of hell if my story could shift just one person's views and move them away from violence.'

Notes

1. I have used the terms victim, perpetrator, survivor and offender more as shorthand to get a message across quickly than for any accurate definition of identity. I also recognize that many perpetrators have been victims and vice versa.

2. Barnes, J. (11 April 2003) 'This war was not worth a child's finger.' *The Guardian.* Available at www.theguardian.com/politics/2003/apr/11/iraq. writersoniraq, accessed on 27 October 2014.

3. Harper, P., and Gray, M. (1997) 'Maps and Meaning in Life and Healing.' In Kedar Nath Dwivedi (ed.) *The Therapeutic Use of Stories.* New York: Routledge, p.51.

4. The Forgiveness Project (2010) 'Ghazi Briegeith & Rami Elhanan (Israel).' Available at http://theforgivenessproject.com/stories/ghazi-briegeith-rami-elhanan-israel, accessed on 27 October 2014.

5. Tutu, D., and Tutu, M. (2014) *The Book of Forgiving*. London: Collins.

6. Tutu, D. *Renew or Release?* Available at http://vimeo.com/94452358, accessed on 27 October 2014.

7. Fraser, G. (11 April 2014) 'Forgiveness is not something that you feel – it is something that you do.' *The Guardian*. Available at www.theguardian.com/commentisfree/belief/2014/apr/11/forgiveness-something-feel-do-rwanda, accessed on 27 October 2014.

8. A term coined by philosopher and law professor Jeffrie Murphy.

9. Wilson, R. (July 2012) 'The futility of forgiveness.' *Prospect Magazine*, p.60.

10. Thomas, L. (12 April 2011) 'We must not forgive too easily, says Archbishop of Canterbury.' *Mail OnLine*. Available at www.dailymail.co.uk/news/article-1375952/We-forgive-easily-says-Archbishop-Canterbury.html, accessed on 27 October 2014.

11. Luskin, F. (2002) *Forgive for Good: A Proven Prescription for Health and Happiness*. New York: HarperCollins.

12. Brown, B. (2010) *The Power of Vulnerability*. Available at https://www.ted.com/talks/brene_brown_on_vulnerability, accessed on 27 October 2010.

13. Chödrön, P. (March 2011) 'Smile at fear.' *Shambhala Sun*, p.45. See also www.lionsroar.com/smile-at-fear-pema-chodrons-teachings-on-bravery-open-heart-basic-goodness, accessed on 27 October 2014.

14. Restorative Justice International (2014). Available at www.restorativejusticeinternational.com/about, accessed on 27 October 2014.

15. Barks, C. (trans.) (2004) *Rumi: Selected Poems*. London: Penguin, p.36.

16. Rilke, R.M. (1962) *Letters to a Young Poet* (trans. Herter Norton). New York: Norton. (Original work published 1934.)

17. al-Berry, K. (2009) *Life is More Beautiful than Paradise: A Jihadist's Own Story*. London: Haus.

18. *Beyond Right & Wrong: Stories of Justice and Forgiveness*. Available at http://beyondrightandwrong.com, accessed on 27 October 2014.

19. Damelin, R. (24 July 2014) 'Shades of Grey Between Israelis and Palestinians.' *The Huffington Post*. Available at www.huffingtonpost.com/robi-damelin/shades-of-grey-between-israel_b_5614967.html, accessed on 27 October 2014.

20. The Forgiveness Project (2010) 'Alistair Little (Northern Ireland).' Available at http://theforgivenessproject.com/stories/alistair-little-northern-ireland, accessed on 27 October 2014.

21. The National Coalition to Abolish the Death Penalty (17 April 2014) 'Breaking News: Tie Vote in New Hampshire Death Penalty Repeal.' Available at www.ncadp.org/blog/entry/breaking-news-tie-vote-in-new-hampshire-death-penalty-repeal, accessed on 27 October 2014.

22. Partington, M. (2012) *If You Sit Very Still*. Bristol: Vala.

23. International Network for Peace (2012) *Guns are Only a Part of the Problem*. Available at http://archive.today/dO6pn, accessed on 27 October 2014.

24. The Forgiveness Project (2010) 'Phyllis Rodriguez & Aicha el-Wafi (USA).' Available at http://theforgivenessproject.com/stories/phyllis-rodriguez-aicha-el-wafi-usa, accessed on 27 October 2014.

25. Cherry, S. (2012) *Healing Agony: Re-imagining Forgiveness*. London: Continuum, p.192.

26. *King Lear*, Act 4, Scene 6.

27. Mitchell, D. (2004) *Cloud Atlas*. London: Hodder and Stoughton.

28. Solzhenitsyn, A. (2003) *The Gulag Archipelago 1918–1956*. London: Harvill, p.75.

29. Ruheman, M. (ed.) (2010) *Letters to Simon*. Bucharest: Simetria, p.43.

30. Zimbardo, P. (2009) *The Lucifer Effect: How Good People Turn Evil*. London: Rider.

31. Nietzsche, F. (2012) *Beyond Good and Evil: Prelude to a Philosophy of the Future*. New York: Courier Dover, p.52.

32. Gobodo-Madikizela, P. (2004) *A Human Being Died That Night: A South African Woman Confronts the Legacy of Apartheid*. New York: Mariner.

Eva Kor

Poland

The day I forgave the Nazis, privately I forgave my parents whom I hated all my life for not having saved me from Auschwitz.

At the age of ten, twins Eva and Miriam Mozes were taken to Auschwitz where Nazi doctor, Josef Mengele, used them for medical experiments. Both survived, but Miriam died in 1993 when she developed cancer of the bladder as a consequence of the experiments done on her as a child. Eva Kor has since spoken explicitly about her experiences at Auschwitz and founded The CANDLES Holocaust Museum in Indiana, USA, where she now lives. In 2003 the museum was destroyed in an arson attack, believed to be organized by white supremacists.

Miriam and I were part of a group of children who were alive for one reason only – to be used as human guinea pigs. During our time in Auschwitz we talked very little. Starved for food and human kindness, it took every ounce of strength just to stay alive. Because we were twins, we were used in a variety of experiments.

Three times a week we'd be placed naked in a room, for 6–8 hours, to be measured and studied. It was unbelievably demeaning.

In another type of experiment they took blood from one arm and gave us injections in the other. After one such injection I became very ill and was taken to the hospital. Dr Mengele came in the next day, looked at my fever chart and declared that I had only two weeks to live. For two weeks I was between life and death but I refused to die. If I had died, Mengele would have given Miriam a lethal injection in order to do a double autopsy. When I didn't die, he carried on experimenting with us and as a result Miriam's kidneys stopped growing. They remained the size of a child's all her life.

On 27 January 1945, four days before my 11th birthday, Auschwitz was liberated by the Soviet army. After nine months in refugee camps I returned to my village in Romania to find that no one from my family had survived.

Echoes from Auschwitz were a part of my life but I did not speak publicly about my experiences until 1978 after the television series *The Holocaust* was aired. People would ask me about the experiments but I couldn't remember very much so I wanted to find other twins who were liberated with me. I wrote to newspapers asking them to publish an appeal for other survivors of Mengele to contact me. By 1980 I was sending out 500 letters a year – but still no response. In desperation, one day I decided to start an organization in which I would make myself President. People are always impressed if they get a letter from a president, and it worked. Finally I was able to find other twin survivors and exchange memories. It was an immensely healing experience.

In 1993 I was invited to lecture to some doctors in Boston and was asked if I could bring a Nazi doctor with me. I thought it was a mad request until I remembered that I'd once been in a documentary which had also featured a Dr Hans Munch from Auschwitz. I contacted him in Germany and he said he would meet with me for a videotaped interview to take to the conference. In July 1993 I was on my way to meet this Nazi doctor. I was so scared but when I arrived at his home he treated me with the utmost respect. I asked him if he'd seen the gas chambers. He said this was a nightmare he dealt with every day of his life. I was surprised that Nazis had nightmares too and asked him if he would come with me to Auschwitz to sign a document at the ruins of the gas chambers. He said that he would love to do it.

In my desperate effort to find a meaningful 'thank you' gift for Dr Munch, I searched the stores, and my heart, for many months. Then the idea of a Forgiveness letter came to my mind. I knew it would be a meaningful gift, but it became a gift to myself as well, because I realized I was NOT a hopeless, powerless victim. When I asked a friend to check my spelling, she challenged me to forgive Dr Mengele too. At first I was adamant that I could never forgive Dr Mengele but then I realized I had the power now…the power to forgive. It was my right to use it. No one could take it away.

On 27 January 1995, at the 50th anniversary of the liberation of Auschwitz, I stood by the ruins of the gas chambers with my children – Dr Alex Kor and Rina Kor – and with Dr Munch and his children and grandchild. Dr Munch signed his document about the operation of the gas chambers while I read my document of forgiveness and signed it. As I did that, I felt a burden of pain was lifted from me. I was no longer in the grip of hate; I was finally free.

The day I forgave the Nazis, privately I forgave my parents whom I hated all my life for not having saved me from Auschwitz. Children expect their parents to protect them; mine couldn't. And then I forgave myself for hating my parents.

Forgiveness is really nothing more than an act of self-healing and self-empowerment. I call it a miracle medicine. It is free, it works and has no side effects.

I believe with every fibre of my being that every human being has the right to live without the pain of the past. For most people there is a big obstacle to forgiveness because society expects revenge. It seems we need to honour our victims but I always wonder if my dead loved ones would want me to live with pain and anger until the end of my life. Some survivors do not want to let go of the pain. They call me a traitor and accuse me of talking in their name. I have never done this. Forgiveness is as personal as chemotherapy – I do it for myself.

www.candlesholocaustmuseum.org

Ray Minniecon

Australia

Healing is a meaningless word for Aboriginal people because we possess a wound that cannot be healed.

Ray Minniecon is an Aboriginal pastor from Australia with roots in the Kabi Kabi nation and Gurang Gurang nation of Queensland. He lives in Sydney and has dedicated his life to supporting members of the Stolen Generations of Aboriginals. The term 'Stolen Generations' refers to the tens of thousands of Aboriginal children who, from the late 1800s until the 1970s, were forcibly removed from their families by government agencies and church missions in an attempt to assimilate them into the culture of white Australia.

As a child I lived in fear. My parents told me that if the police tried to pick us up we should run like crazy. There were times when the black Government car would come into the missions and I'd hear women screaming from one end of the community to the other for us children to run into the bush and hide. I was one of the lucky ones who never got caught.

My father was a Christian leader who worked as a cane cutter and this gave him permission to work on cane farms throughout Queensland. So we would move with him from farm to farm, and when the cane season finished we lived back on the designated reserves or missions. In those days Aboriginal people weren't allowed into the towns.

The Aboriginal Protection Acts (which didn't protect us at all) gave the police the authority to remove Aboriginal children from their families and put them in institutional facilities or foster homes. These children later became known as the Stolen Generations and were subjected to abuse of every possible kind.

Aboriginal people had no recognition. We had never been officially counted in the census, so no one knew exactly how many Aboriginal people or massacres there had been. The government had control over every aspect of our life. We had to live on church missions and reserves; we weren't allowed out after 6pm; we could not mix with white people. The government would determine if we could marry and whom we could marry, how much money we had and who we could work for. We were also restricted in our capacity to get involved in any political agendas and forbidden to speak our languages or practise our traditional cultures.

Then in 1967 there was a National Referendum, called the 'Yes' Vote, when Australians voted overwhelmingly to amend the constitution to include Aboriginal people in the census and give the Federal Government the power to manage Aboriginal affairs. The vote was supposed to make us all equal citizens, and although it did bring an end to the era of forced removals, it created a different set of problems. As we came out of these reserves, missions, institutions and foster homes, we were forced to live in new urban environments where we now had to face the daily onslaught of racism. I joined the rest of the young people who didn't have the wherewithal to counteract this racism and, like them, found the only way to relieve the pain was to get drunk and take drugs. It also gave a false sense of freedom for us. Living without restrictions meant for the first time we could do whatever we wanted to do.

My parents were also struggling with these issues but what kept them together was my father's incredible faith, and eventually I felt the call to follow in his footsteps and leave behind the drug-induced state I was so enjoying. I knew I had to draw back into his faith to find a different direction for my life. That's when I became politically activated. I did eight years of studying which gave me access to the records and stories of my people. I learnt about injustices that few members of my community knew about because we hadn't had proper access to a good education. We were blinded to the cruel actions of the Government which had been implemented with impunity.

Once I graduated I was headhunted to work in the non-government sector because I was one of the few Aboriginals with a degree in that field, but I decided I wanted to work on the streets, at the grass roots where the greatest need lay. The terrible pain you still see on the streets shows how the brutality of our history is continuing into the present.

Many times I've witnessed a white Australian ask a Stolen Generations member for their forgiveness, and the Stolen Generations person will then look them straight in the eye and say, 'You can't apologize if you weren't directly responsible. The Government knew what they were doing. They are the guilty ones.'

There was a national apology. Kevin Rudd, the Australian Prime Minister in 2008, apologized on behalf of all Australians following a national 'Sorry' movement. Whilst many of the promises the Government made have not been implemented, it pricked the conscience of a nation and was a turning point. When someone says 'I'm sorry', then something changes in your spirit.

Healing is a meaningless word for Aboriginal people because we possess a wound that cannot be healed. Rape of the soul is so profound – and particularly for the Stolen Generations who were forcibly removed from their parents, families, communities and culture. You can't put a band-aid on that. You can't take a pill. For these people the concept of healing and the concept of forgiveness is difficult and challenging. Reconciliation only happens when you're restored in your own spirit. That's why we prefer to talk about social and emotional and psychological well-being. If you fix the psyche and restore well-being through a process of reconnection and reconstruction of identity, then you have a platform for someone to deal with intergenerational and historical pain and be a human being again. Only then can someone have an opportunity to receive or express forgiveness.

I struggle with forgiveness but I know I have to practise it every day to relieve my bitterness. It's a moment-by-moment thing because I can walk into a shop and have a person do racist acts without even knowing they are racist. And when that happens, I have to walk away and deal with my rage and anger, and learn to say, 'OK Ray, forgive that person.' If I didn't forgive, then the pain of the past would always be present.

Jayne Stewart

England

*Can I forgive him
for something
he denies?*

Jayne Stewart and her brother were sexually abused by their father for many years. He denies that the abuse ever happened. As an adult, Jayne cut off all contact with her father, but in 1998 she decided to get back in touch with him and has continued to dialogue despite irreconcilable differences. Tragically, in 1999, Jayne's brother committed suicide.

I was sexually abused by my father from when I was three until I was 12. I only survived the abuse by disassociating – my body stayed present but my conscious mind split off and 'forgot'. But when my son was three, I began to recover my memories and in the end decided to confront my father. He denied the abuse and continues to do so. I survived the remembering, by splitting in a different way – I stopped all contact with my father.

At least that is the situation from my perspective; from my father's perspective it looks very different. Out of the blue comes a false accusation of childhood sexual abuse, first from his daughter and then from his son. They cut off from him completely and deny him access to his grandchildren. He is reported to social services and questioned by the police. His son sends vindictive letters to him, his second wife and to members of his local community. He is afraid that he may lose his job, his second family and his place as a respected member of church and community. His son commits suicide and he is blamed and not allowed to go to the funeral.

Reconnecting with my father has not been an easy journey. For a long time I focused on my rage. I wanted revenge, to punish, even to kill. I made my father wholly bad, and 'Other'. But I wasn't able to cut myself off totally. I began to grieve that this abuse was done to me not by a stranger, but by someone who also loved me, and I loved him.

I first decided to get back in touch with my father after a 5Rhythms Dance Workshop at which I realized I was trapped by the past and unable to move beyond feeling a powerless victim. That first meeting was a very positive experience. I told my father I had not changed what I believed, only what I was choosing to do with it. I was no longer a helpless victim, I made choices, I set boundaries and I spoke directly about my experience of the abuse, all things which were not possible as a child.

I invited my father to speak from within his belief system and asked him to allow me to do the same. I told him I knew that not all of what happened between us when I was a child was bad and that I also wanted to acknowledge the good bits. I suggested going for a walk and he agreed. Walking, we began to explore ways of communicating across our irreconcilable differences and have been doing so ever since.

Over the last eight years, fighting to establish the truth of what happened between us in the past has become less important to me than what happens now and in the future. At first when I started speaking out about my abuse, it was very important to me to be believed. Now I am less concerned about establishing my truth and more interested in how to relate positively across our irreconcilable differences. I spent a long time hating my father; now I am finding more creative ways to relate to him beyond the victim/perpetrator polarity. Making the shift beyond feeling a helpless victim of an unchangeable abuser is an awesome experience and has been personally healing both psychologically and spiritually.

In addition, when I am aware that this most private of oppressions between father and daughter is also part of a much bigger picture and that all of these issues relate not only to sexual abuse but also to all of the abuses that we perpetrate in the world, I feel less alone and more inspired to create something meaningful from my traumatic experiences that will also be healing for the world. I hope that together we can find new ways of resolving our conflicts that do not perpetuate cycles of revenge and violence, whether those conflicts are with our friends and family or carried out in our names by our political leaders or in the names of our spiritual traditions.

It is not an easy step to go beyond the polarity of victim and perpetrator; we tend to act as if the innocent and the guilty are totally separate. But victim and perpetrator, 'good' and 'bad', co-exist within each of us. My father was a good son to my grandmother, he is a well-respected member of his local community and he was both a good and an abusive father. Suicide bombers may also be good sons and fathers and well-respected members of their local communities.

Forgiveness is an interesting concept in relation to my father. I think forgiving is an ongoing process, which comes and goes and develops over time, rather than something that can be achieved once and for all. He says he has forgiven me for all the upset I have caused him by my 'false accusation'. Can I forgive him for something he denies? The answer is both No and Yes. What my father did to me and to my brother is unforgivable, but I no longer need him to admit it or to pay for it in some way. I have reached a new place, a place beyond my painful history and towards a more sustainable future both for myself in my personal relationships and, I hope, for the world.

This story is not told in my own name; originally that decision was made for legal reasons. This is a charged issue: childhood sexual abuse is still such a taboo subject, and there is often a strong prohibition against telling anyone. Many of us keep silent for years, as the high-profile celebrity cases in the UK demonstrated. So whilst the abused child part of me feels relieved not to be identified, the writer/warrior/activist part feels aggrieved not to be able to stand proudly behind her words and actions.

Recently, however, a new thread is emerging: *choosing* not to use my own name in order to protect family members, including my father. Considering the impact my actions may have on others is one way I can bring in what was missing during the abuse, and is something we need to practise globally if we are to survive.

http://uncommongroundkjc.wordpress.com

Bud Welch

USA

'I have to do something different, because what I'm doing isn't working.'

In April 1995 Bud Welch's 23-year-old daughter, Julie Marie, was killed in the bombing of the Murrah Federal Building in Oklahoma City along with 167 others. In the months after her death, Bud changed from supporting the death penalty for Timothy McVeigh and Terry Nichols to taking a public stand against it. In 2001 Timothy McVeigh was executed for his part in the bombing.

Three days after the bombing, as I watched Tim McVeigh being led out of the courthouse, I hoped someone in a high building with a rifle would shoot him dead. I wanted him to fry. In fact, I'd have killed him myself if I'd had the chance.

Unable to deal with the pain of Julie's death, I started self-medicating with alcohol until eventually the hangovers were lasting all day. Then, on a cold day in January 1996, I came to the bomb site – as I did every day – and I looked across the wasteland where the

Murrah Building once stood. My head was splitting from drinking the night before and I thought, 'I have to do something different, because what I'm doing isn't working.'

For the next few weeks I started to reconcile things in my mind, and finally concluded that it was revenge and hate that had killed Julie and the 167 others. Tim McVeigh and Terry Nichols had been against the US government for what happened in Waco, Texas, in 1993, and seeing what they'd done with their vengeance, I knew I had to send mine in a different direction. Shortly afterwards I started speaking out against the death penalty.

I also remembered that shortly after the bombing I'd seen a news report on Tim McVeigh's father, Bill. He was shown stooping over a flowerbed, and when he stood up I could see that he'd been physically bent over in pain. I recognized it because I was feeling that pain, too.

In December 1998, after Tim McVeigh had been sentenced to death, I had a chance to meet Bill McVeigh at his home near Buffalo. I wanted to show him that I did not blame him. His youngest daughter, Jennifer, also wanted to meet me, and after Bill had showed me his garden, the three of us sat around the kitchen table. Up on the wall were family snapshots, including Tim's graduation picture. They noticed that I kept looking up at it, so I felt compelled to say something. 'God, what a good-looking kid,' I said.

Earlier, when we'd been in the garden, Bill had asked me, 'Bud, are you able to cry?' I'd told him, 'I don't usually have a problem crying.' His reply was, 'I can't cry, even though I've got a lot to cry about.' But now, sitting at the kitchen table, looking at Tim's photo, a big tear rolled down his face. It was the love of a father for a son.

When I got ready to leave, I shook Bill's hand, then extended it to Jennifer, but she just grabbed me and threw her arms around me. She was the same sort of age as Julie but felt so much taller. I don't know which one of us started crying first. Then I held her face in my hands and said, 'Look, honey, the three of us are in this for the rest of our lives. I don't want your brother to die and I'll do everything I can to prevent it.' As I walked away from the house, I realized that until that moment I had walked alone, but now a tremendous weight had lifted from my shoulders. I had found someone who was a bigger victim of the Oklahoma bombing than I was, because while I can speak in front of thousands of people and say wonderful things about Julie, if Bill McVeigh meets a stranger he probably doesn't even say he had a son.

About a year before the execution I found it in my heart to forgive Tim McVeigh. It was a release for me rather than for him.

Six months after the bombing a poll taken in Oklahoma City of victims' families and survivors showed that 85 per cent wanted the death penalty for Tim McVeigh. Six years later that figure had dropped to nearly half, and now most of those who supported his execution have come to believe it was a mistake. In other words, they didn't feel any better after Tim McVeigh was taken from his cell and killed.

John Carter

England

Meeting with me allowed her to put a face to her fear.

John Carter got involved in crime at the age of 12. After eight years in prison he finally got to meet one of his victims at a restorative justice victim-offender meeting. He is currently working as a gardener and lives in Shropshire with his partner.

My life of crime started at an early age. By the time I was 14 I had various juvenile convictions which carried on throughout my teenage years and even when I left school and took up an apprenticeship in engineering. But it was joining a Hell's Angel motorcycle gang that led me into more serious crime. For once I felt an overwhelming sense of belonging. It seemed to me that this way – the violence, theft and robbery – was the path to follow.

By the age of 22 I had received an eight-year prison sentence for armed robbery with a date for release in five years' time. I was adamant I wasn't going to stay in prison that long, so I escaped twice during that time which added several years to my sentence and meant that I ended up in solitary confinement at Dartmoor prison. It was here that I became even more violent. I disrespected everyone around me, especially the prison authorities, and reached the lowest point in my life. It was during this period that I was assessed for psychiatric evaluation and eventually found myself at the therapeutic prison, Grendon Underwood. On arrival the reception officer informed me his name was Derek and he would be my personal officer. I almost collapsed because no prison officer had ever spoken to me like that before. It showed me I could perhaps trust someone in authority.

At Grendon the whole unit was run on the guidelines of group therapy. Meetings were held to debate and understand criminal behaviour and a lot of soul searching went on. I did exceedingly well in therapy working on myself and ultimately helping others until eventually I was given the opportunity to have part of my sentence reduced. Instead of being happy about this, I suddenly found myself feeling anxious and realized I feared being released. I questioned whether the work I'd done on myself would be enough to encourage me not to reoffend. Then a probation officer told me about restorative justice – a process that could help me understand empathy and compassion. Restorative justice was almost completely unheard of back in 1988 and had certainly never been undertaken in any British prison, but I felt the only course of action would be to go through this process.

My probation officer then asked me: 'Which one of your victims do you believe will have suffered the most from your actions?' I had to think hard as there were so many victims. I then remembered a pub brawl incident which I'd started and where I'd injured various people including a girl of 18. My actions on that evening resulted in her being scarred for life. My victim was tracked down and, six years after the event, she agreed to meet me, along with her parents.

When I walked into the visiting room, I noticed the young woman had a prominent six-inch scar on the side of her face. I had no idea who she was but I felt this deep bond between us because we'd shared something; something which for her was, of course, entirely negative. We both sat there and looked at each other across the table. I could see she was full of rage. It was highly traumatic. Her father was clenching his fists, her mother looked distraught. I was the first to speak, and for the first time I found I was able express exactly how I'd felt at the moment of the offence. It was the first time I felt the reality of the hurt that I'd caused, not only to her but to her family too.

She then took me through what had happened to her that night, about how she'd gone out with friends from college, how she'd had a couple of drinks and then she noticed me and just knew something terrible was going to happen. She also spoke about how that event had affected her ever since. Towards the end of the meeting we all broke down and cried. Finally I told her how remorseful I felt and then, after a brief pause, she said, 'I forgive you.' I hadn't asked for this and certainly didn't expect it, but those words had a profound effect on me. They gave me the resolve to not steal and to certainly not commit violence against another person ever again. As for my victim, the meeting with me allowed her to put a face to her fear and hopefully reassured her that it would never happen again.

This meeting completely restructured my whole life. I was released from prison in 1990 and set about building a life, a family and a future. And yes, there have been difficult times, but despite these I have never returned to a life of crime. The adrenaline rush and excitement I craved as a young man is now satisfied by mountain biking and kayaking, and I can now forge meaningful and positive relationships with people who know nothing about my past. I feel the whole restorative justice process and meeting my victim changed me forever. I now feel eternally grateful to my victim and hope that she has found the happiness in her life that I eventually found in mine.

Ginn Fourie and Letlapa Mphahlele

South Africa

By meeting together we are able to restore each other's humanity.

In 1993 Lyndi Fourie was killed in the Heidelberg Tavern Massacre in Cape Town, aged 23. Nine years later, her mother, Ginn Fourie, heard a radio interview with the man who had ordered the attack. Letlapa Mphahlele, the former Director of Operations of the Azanian People's Liberation Army (APLA), the military wing of the Pan Africanist Congress (PAC), was in Cape Town to promote his biography, *Child of this Soil*. Since then both have been working to further conciliation in South Africa through the Lyndi Fourie Foundation. Ginn and Letlapa also feature in the documentary feature *Beyond Forgiving*.

Ginn Fourie

On the evening of 30 December 1993, a hail of AK-47 gunfire ended our daughter's life and dreams. Lyndi had no time to debate why the PAC wanted white people to suffer as black people had suffered under apartheid, even though she had often wept at the many injustices that black people had endured.

As parents, we struggled to come to terms with our loss. It was a time of deep agony for me, my husband and our son, Anthony. At the funeral my eldest brother, who conducted the service, recommended that the most appropriate Christian response to violence is to absorb it, just as Lyndi's soft body had done on that fateful day.

Within a week of the Heidelberg Massacre three young men were detained, and in November 1994 they stood trial. I sat in the Supreme Court in Cape Town, looking at them in the dock: Humphrey Gqomfa, Vuyisile Madasi and Zola Mabala. As I did so, I was confronted by my own feelings of anger and sadness, but somehow I could engender no hate. During the trial I sent a message to them via the interpreter which said, 'If they are guilty or feel guilty, I forgive them.'

However, I also depended on the law to avenge my loss, and I was relieved when all three were convicted of murder and sent to prison for an average of 25 years each. The Judge described them as puppets: puppets who had carried out a violent crime which had been orchestrated by more cunning and intelligent people than themselves.

Many could not countenance my forgiveness for Lyndi's killers, but as a Christian I cherished the memory of Christ forgiving his murderers. Since then I have come to understand forgiveness as a process which involves the principled decision to give up your justifiable right to revenge. Because to accept violation is a devaluation of the self.

At the Truth and Reconciliation Commission (TRC; www.justice.gov.za/trc) hearing in October 1997, I learnt that Lyndi's killers were likely to be granted amnesty, and I did not oppose this. At the conclusion of the hearings the three young men asked to speak to me. They thanked me and said that they would take my message of forgiveness and hope to their communities and to their graves, whether they received amnesty or not.

Then, in October 2002, I turned on my car radio and heard an interview with Letlapa Mphahlele – the man who had master-minded the Heidelberg massacre. I knew he had been dodging the public prosecutor and had not applied for amnesty, and so with a sense of anger and righteous indignation I took myself down to his book launch.

During the event I stood up and asked him whether he was trivializing the TRC process by not taking part in it. To my surprise, he responded in a very positive way. He said he could understand why people might think this, but that in his view the TRC had trivialized the fact that APLA were fighting a just war. And why, he asked, while his soldiers were being held in prison, had the apartheid defence forces been spared? I hadn't thought of it like this before, and I welled up with tears. Then Letlapa came straight from the podium to where I was sitting and said, 'I'll do anything if you'll meet with me this week.' In that moment I saw remorse in his eyes. It would have been so much easier if he had been a monster with horns and a tail.

People said he was unapologetic, but I soon discovered that for Letlapa saying 'sorry' is too easy. He wants to build bridges between our communities to bring conciliation. That October he invited me to his homecoming ceremony and asked me to make a speech. It was here that I was able to apologize to his people for the shame and humiliation which my ancestors had brought on them through slavery, colonialism and apartheid. Vulnerable feelings, when expressed to other people, have the potential to establish lasting bonds.

Letlapa's name means 'man of stone' and I feel that he has been weathered by a formidable struggle to become a 'child of this soil'. I too am a child of this soil. I know his comrades' bullets killed my daughter, and that terrible pain will always be with me. But I have forgiven the man who gave the command. I feel his humanity.

Letlapa Mphahlele

I am an atheist but I believe absolutely in reconciliation, meeting soul to soul, person to person. As human beings, we have to face each other and mend relationships. Getting to know Ginn has been a profound and humbling experience for me. From our first meeting in 2002, Ginn understood me. While others couldn't understand why these terrorists were still unapologetic, Ginn said that she detected remorse in me. By this time all the charges against me had been withdrawn, but still I felt nothing inside. It was only when people extended gifts of forgiveness that the roots of my heart were shaken, and something was restored inside me.

Since meeting Ginn, I've had to face the fact that people were killed because of my orders. I've also had to acknowledge that the people we fought and harmed and caused to grieve were never our direct enemies. I believed that terror had to be answered with terror, and I authorized high-profile massacres on white civilians in the same way that our oppressors had done to us. At the time it seemed the only valid response. But where would it have ended? If my enemies had been cannibals, would I have eaten white flesh? If my enemies had raped black women, would I have raped white women?

I have changed since that time and I no longer believe you should meet violence with violence. I now think you can deal with oppression in a more creative way. I believe what Ginn says, that even if violence comes your way, you should 'absorb it'. And that is not the coward's way; it's extremely difficult to do.

My mission now is to reach out to those who survived, because by meeting together we are able to restore each other's humanity.

When Ginn attended my homecoming, she delivered the most moving speech of the day. She stood up and asked for forgiveness on behalf of her ancestors. She also got the loudest applause – louder than I got after nearly two decades in exile.

Some people have decided not to forgive me for what I have done, and I understand that. It's not easy to forgive, but to those who have forgiven I believe that this is how we start to rebuild our communities. This is an intense human mission. People sometimes ask me if I have also killed people myself, with my own hands. When I am asked this, I never answer. Not because I am afraid of speaking the truth, but because I believe that every foot soldier who killed at my command is less guilty than me, because I authorized the targets. I exonerate those who pulled the trigger. It is I who should shoulder the blame.

www.lyndifouriefoundation.org.za

Bassam Aramin

Palestine

I tried to hide my tears from the other prisoners: they wouldn't have understood why I was crying about the pain of my oppressors.

Bassam Aramin became involved in the Palestinian struggle as a boy growing up in the ancient city of Hebron. At 17, he was caught planning an attack on Israeli troops and spent the next seven years in prison. In 2005 he co-founded Combatants for Peace, an organization of former Israeli and Palestinian combatants leading a non-violent struggle against the occupation. Since then Bassam has remained a peace activist – even when, two years later, his ten-year-old daughter Abir was gunned down and killed by an Israeli soldier.

As a child I fought the occupation by raising the Palestinian flag in our playground. We never felt safe. We were always running from jeeps to avoid the soldiers beating us. Our homes were invaded and children were killed. At the age of 12 I joined a demonstration where a boy was shot by a soldier. I watched him die in front of me.

From that moment I developed a deep need for revenge. I became part of a group whose mission was to get rid of the catastrophe that had come to our town. We called ourselves freedom fighters, but the outside world called us terrorists. At first we just threw stones and empty bottles, but when we came across some discarded hand-grenades in a cave, we decided to hurl them at the Israeli jeeps. Two of them exploded. No one was injured but we were caught and in 1985, at the age of 17, I received a seven-year prison sentence.

In prison we were treated like heroes by the other prisoners, but our jailers taught us how to continue hating and resisting. On 1 October 1987, 120 of us – all teenage boys – were waiting to go into the dining room when the alarms suddenly went off. Over a hundred armed soldiers then suddenly appeared and ordered us to strip naked. They beat us until we could hardly stand. I was held the longest and beaten the hardest. What struck me was that all the soldiers wore smiles on their faces. They were beating us without hatred, because for them this was just a training exercise and they saw us as objects.

As I was being beaten, I remembered a movie I'd seen the year before about the Holocaust. At the time I'd been happy that Hitler had killed six million Jews. I remember wishing that he'd killed them all, because then I would never have been sent to prison. But some minutes into the movie, I found myself crying and feeling angry that the Jews were being herded into gas chambers without fighting back. If they knew they were going to die, why didn't they scream out? I tried to hide my tears from the other prisoners: they wouldn't have understood why I was crying about the pain of my oppressors. It was the first time I felt empathy.

So now, walking between the soldiers who were beating me, I remembered the movie and I started screaming out at them: 'Murderers! Nazis! Oppressors!' And as a consequence, I felt no pain.

The incident with the soldiers made me realize that we had to preserve our humanity – our right to laugh and our right to cry – in order to save ourselves. I also slowly realized that the Israeli oppression was because of the Holocaust, and I decided to try to understand who the Jews were. This led to a conversation with a prison guard. The guards all thought of us as terrorists and we hated them, but this guard asked me, 'How can someone quiet like you become a terrorist?' I replied, 'No, you're the terrorist. I'm a freedom fighter.' He really believed that we, the Palestinians, were the settlers, not the Israelis. I said, 'If you can convince me that we are the settlers, then I'll declare this in front of all the prisoners.'

It was the start of a dialogue and a friendship. We discovered many similarities and some months later the guard said he understood now that we were not the settlers. He even became a supporter of the Palestinian struggle. From then on he always treated us with respect, and once even smuggled in two big bottles of Coca Cola, which I shared with all the other prisoners. Seeing how this transformation happened through dialogue and without force made me realize that the only way to peace was through non-violence. Our dialogue enabled us both to see each other's purity of heart and good intent.

When I was released, it was the time of the Oslo Accords, and there was a great feeling of hope for a two-state solution. But it never happened because the politicians said we weren't ready for it. I think if I hadn't had such strong beliefs and principles, anger would have taken over. It wasn't until 2005 that some of us who believed in non-violence started meeting in secret with former Israeli soldiers. We were meeting as true enemies who wanted to speak. The Israelis were refusing to fight, not for the sake of the Palestinian people, but for the sake of the morals of their society. We too were not acting to save Israeli lives, but to prevent our society from suffering more. It was only later that we both came to feel a responsibility for each other's people.

There is a much darker side to my story. On 16 January 2007, my ten-year-old daughter, Abir, was shot and killed in cold blood by a member of the Israeli border police while standing outside her school with some classmates. There were no demonstrations or violence or intifada. I have been appalled by the details of what happened, not least that she had just bought a candy at the store and hadn't had time to eat it.

It took me four and a half years to prove in the civil court that my daughter had been killed with a rubber bullet. My goal has been to bring the soldier responsible to trial, but the Supreme Court decided after four and a half years there is no evidence, so they closed the file for the fourth time. I believe in justice and many hundreds of my Israeli brothers and Jewish brothers around the world support me. I want to bring this man to justice because he killed my ten-year-old daughter; not because he's an Israeli and I'm a Palestinian but because my child was not a fighter, nor was she a Fatah or Hamas member. For there to be reconciliation, and for me to consider forgiveness, Israel has to recognize such crimes.

Abir's murder could have led me down the easy path of hatred and vengeance, but for me there was no return from dialogue and non-violence. After all, it was one Israeli soldier who shot my daughter, but one hundred former Israeli soldiers who built a garden in her name at the school where she was murdered.

www.combatantsforpeace.org
www.theparentscircle.com

Madeleine Black

England

I used to think that they were evil, but I started to understand that they didn't come into this world that way.

Madeleine Black is a counsellor and lives in Glasgow. Growing up in London in the late 1970s, she was brutally raped at the age of 13 by two American teenagers. In 2014, having come to terms with how the trauma had shaped her life, she decided to share her story publicly for the first time.

When I was 13, in a flat belonging to my friend's mother, who was away for the weekend, I was attacked by two teenage American students. They held a knife to my throat and tortured and raped me many times over, for about four or five hours. I begged them to stop, but they just kicked me and laughed at me. I remember wishing they would kill me to make it all end.

During the event I became aware of a young Tibetan monk in burgundy robes and an orange shawl by my right-hand side. I was also aware that I had floated out of my body and was on top of the wardrobe watching what was happening to me down below. The monk was praying next to my body and telling me I was going to be OK. He covered up my naked body with his orange shawl and calmed me down.

Near to the end, one of my attackers urinated and out of everything they did that night this felt the worst; it was one of the images that haunted me for years to come. Before they left, the most violent of the pair punched me in the chest, held the knife to my throat again and said if I told anyone he would find me and kill me. I believed him.

After that I remember waking up with my friend in the bed next to me. I thought the noise of her bracelets were keys in the door and was worried that my attackers were coming back. I was covered in vomit, excrement and blood.

We then spent the morning tidying up the flat and decided we shouldn't tell anyone as we weren't meant to be there and we had been drinking. It was now Sunday morning and we went back to school the next day as if nothing had happened.

I lived in fear that the two young men who had raped me would kill me one day. I felt worthless, totally degraded and empty. I thought it was all my fault, and most of all I felt so dirty and contaminated. I would spend ages in the bath for many years afterwards scrubbing my skin with cleaning products.

I started to become very promiscuous as I had no self-respect, and if a boy approached me, I just let him do whatever he wanted because I thought if I resisted he would hurt me. At the same time I started drinking and taking drugs. I also stopped eating as that was the only thing I felt I could control.

It became so painful to be alive that one night I took as many of my mum's pills as I could find and ended up in a children's psychiatric ward where I spent the next six months. During that time no one ever asked if anything had happened to me, even though I was clearly traumatized.

When I was about 16, I told my mum about the rape by writing down what had happened and leaving it on my pillow before I went to school one day. My parents phoned my friend's mum, but my friend denied it all and said it had never happened like I said. My dad didn't believe her and wanted to go to the police, but I begged him not to as I thought it was my fault and that my attackers would come back and kill me. I couldn't believe what my friend had said.

I have often wondered what happened to my friend who was also with me that night, and I have to accept that I honestly don't know. We had both been drinking heavily too and she was put into another bedroom in the flat. It was the first time I had ever tried alcohol. The only outcomes I can assume are that she was also raped and blocked it out or nothing happened to her and she passed out. When I reflect back to how she reacted when her mum was called by my parents, either scenario could fit.

I left school at 16 and my parents thought it would be a good idea for me to get away, so when I was 17 I went to Israel for a year where I worked on a kibbutz and then spent time in Ashkelon, which is where I met my husband.

I believe meeting him saved my life, as I was on a path of self-destruction; he loved me and made me feel worthwhile again. I used to drive him mad by constantly asking him why he loved me. When we talked about starting a family, I always told him I couldn't or didn't want children. In my head I thought that giving birth would be like being raped again.

After a while, though, I decided that I didn't want my rapists to take that part of my life away and I had to do this to heal myself. My revenge would be leading a good and happy life.

When my eldest daughter was nearly 13, I started to have lots of flashbacks. I had nightmares for about three years which would wake me up and I could feel the presence of the young men in the room and at times could feel their weight on my body. But the monk was always beside me too.

Around this time I was doing a psychotherapy course, and I knew it was now time to talk about what had happened. I realized the only way to stop driving myself insane with all the memories that were flooding in was to come to terms with the rape and accept it for what it was. After all, I had survived it and it wasn't happening anymore.

Most of my life, I hated the men who raped me and wished them a slow, painful death. However, as I was working with my therapist, something happened that I never set out to do and that was I chose to forgive them. I used to think that they were evil, but I started to understand that they didn't come into this world that way. They were born just like me as an innocent baby, and then I started to wonder how they knew to be so violent and cruel to another human at such a young age. It made me think they couldn't have had the best of lives and had witnessed or experienced violence themselves.

I also realized that they wouldn't know if I felt hate toward them and the only person it was hurting was me. I can honestly say that I have no fear, hate or revenge in my heart towards them anymore. I know that, whatever they did to me, they can never touch the real essence of me and who I am. I am very lucky as I rebuilt my life, have a beautiful family and feel so grateful to be alive. I have come to realize that for them to live with the guilt of what they did must be so much harder than for me to live with the harm they inflicted on me.

Sammy Rangel

USA

*I went into prison
as a street punk
and came out as a
brutal leader with
a killer mentality.*

Sammy Rangel spent most of his early years in mental institutions, foster homes and detention homes. He embraced violence at the age of 11, joining the Maniac Latin Disciples gang and spending long periods in prison. It wasn't until a drug abuse programme helped him rehabilitate that Sammy began to further his education and start working for a Safe Streets outreach programme in Wisconsin. Today, with a Masters in Social Work, he consults with law enforcement agencies and other service providers on reducing violent extremism. He has written an autobiography, *Fourbears: The Myths of Forgiveness*, and is founder of Formers Anonymous, a self-help programme for men and women looking to exit a lifestyle of crime and violence.

It started aged three when my sister and I were raped by my mother's brother. Even as a three-year-old you know when something terribly wrong is happening to you. I was also systematically and sadistically abused by my mother and stepfather throughout my childhood. My mother's abuse was physical and it was aimed only at me, not at my sister or my two younger brothers. I was singled out as the outcast in the family.

My mother would always harm me in the worst possible way – so if it was a belt she was using, she'd hit me with the buckle end. I seldom got fed and had to sneak or steal food, and she didn't let me lie down at night; she made me kneel by her bed until I keeled over. She did everything she could do to degrade me. My siblings, who were conditioned to ignore me, just turned a blind eye. By the age of eight I tried to hang myself – only failing because the extension lead broke.

The day I decided to run away was also the day I almost killed my mother. I stood over her in bed with a knife, but aged 11 I didn't have the strength or the courage to go through with it. After that I spent most of my early teenage years on the street. I joined a gang, started drinking and smoking cocaine, and having lots of sex. I was still 11 when I lost my first baby.

The shit that had happened at home turned my heart really hard – to a level where I didn't give a fuck. One of the older gang members asked me to slit a guy's throat and, when I said I couldn't, he showed me how to do it. Soon it didn't matter what I did. By now I was violent and aggressive to the extreme.

At 17 I went to prison for the first time. Even though I was a father, with one child and another on the way, I was excited about going to prison because I knew it was where I could gain power and authority. And so the gang fighting that had started on the outside crystallized in prison. Now I had an ideology where violence was glamorized and glorified. It gave my life a sense of meaning and legitimized everything I did.

I became so bad that I ended up being sent to a maximum security prison where the inmates ran the establishment. I belonged to a Puerto Rican gang but it was the white racist gang members who were in charge. It was here that I got caught up in a race riot which involved shootings, stabbings and hostage taking.

I went into prison as a street punk and came out as a brutal leader with a killer mentality. I started walking the streets with both a gun and a shank. I'd tell people I was more animal than man. Seven months later I was back in for armed robbery and again immediately put in the segregation hole.

The first small change happened when this man called George came to the hole to talk to me one day. He confused me by calling me 'nephew' and saying he wanted to see me in his office. I'd had no human contact for months and yet he got me brought from my cell to his office – which required four men putting me in shackles, handcuffs and chains – and then he told the guards to take off my chains. I couldn't believe it: it was like letting a werewolf loose on a herd of sheep. It shocked me that this guy, who was half my size, wasn't afraid of me. And then he asked me for my story – and I told him the whole thing. He didn't flinch or pity me – he just listened. Afterwards he said: 'I want to help you get out of this place.' I left knowing I'd been affected in some way. The meeting had left me feeling vulnerable.

A year later I beat up four guards and I felt bad because I didn't want to do that anymore. I wrote to George and told him I'd 'fucked up'. I expected him to be upset with me, but he just said, 'You don't owe me anything.' Because he wasn't disappointed in me, it gave me hope to carry on.

It was on an intense drug rehabilitation programme that I made my change. I had to talk about my life, and my mother, which unleashed a torrent of emotion. I cried so much my face looked as if it was covered in bruises. When a fellow inmate told me that I didn't love my daughter because I hadn't properly tried to find her, that hurt terribly because I knew it was the truth. In an instant I went from feeling self-pity to feeling remorse. In fact, it was the first time I'd experienced empathy.

From that moment I did everything to try to put my life together. When I left prison, I decided I needed to find forgiveness from my son and daughter, and also to forgive my mother and everyone else who had hurt me – including her brother. I had created myths as to why I couldn't forgive my mother – the myth that she must accept my forgiveness, that she didn't deserve it, and most of all that what she had done was unforgivable. I realized now that I needed to let go of these myths because as long as I tried to collect what my mother owed me, I would never move forward in my life. And so, in the end, it was forgiveness that released me from the hate that was consuming me.

https://www.facebook.com/RacineFormersAnonymous

Anne Marie Hagan

Canada

*Forgiveness is
not permission.
It doesn't mean
that you agree
with what the
offender has done.*

**Anne Marie Hagan's father, Thomas Hagan, was 56 years old
when he was murdered in 1979 in the little fishing village of
Kingman's Cove, Newfoundland, Canada. He received 16 axe
cuts, several in the head, neck and face. The 30-year-old man
who committed the act was his neighbour. He was suffering
from schizophrenia, and he believed that he'd heard the voice
of his dead mother telling him to kill Thomas Hagan.**

It was Sunday 12 August 1979. I was a 19-year-old nursing student
home on summer holidays when I saw my father murdered with
an axe. I tried to stop the man, but he axed me as well.

Filled with sadness and despair, I became completely consumed
with anger, bitterness, vengeance and self-pity. I was absolutely
determined that this man would never, ever regain his freedom.
The longer he was locked away, the greater the value of my
father's life.

Then, on 7 June 1996, during a comprehensive campaign I'd organized to stop his release, I talked with him face-to-face. It was during this meeting, while learning more about him as a human being and the horrendous suffering that he'd endured, that everything changed.

I'd not heard of the term 'restorative justice' then, but in that face-to-face meeting, which lasted one hour and 40 minutes, 16 years and ten months of misery was just wiped away. As he started to cry and said, 'I'm to blame, I'm to blame', I couldn't take it anymore. I rushed around the table and hugged him, telling him that I forgave him. I remember saying to him, 'Blame is too strong a word, blame is too strong a word.'

I could never have imagined that in doing so I would set myself free. Finally I was able to let go of all the pain and torment that had held me captive, realizing that I'd been my own jailer. My life changed as I began to see the world through new eyes. I felt joy again; the numbness was gone.

After his release my father's killer found work and he has rebuilt his life. I admire him for having the strength and the courage to do so. I would advocate for him if the need ever arises. He and I have talked at length about what happened on that fateful day, and how my forgiving him has changed both our lives.

In June 2002, my journey as a motivational speaker began. Since then I've spoken to thousands of people across Canada and the United States, including police officers and prison inmates. Before I forgave my father's killer I had zero compassion for such people. Now, I see each inmate as somebody's child.

Forgiveness is not permission. It doesn't mean that you agree with what the offender has done, or that they had a right to do what they did. Also, forgiveness cannot be conditional on remorse because that would mean we can only forgive those who are sorry. Forgiveness is recognizing that the offender is a human being who is deserving of kindness, compassion and love despite the harm they have done.

In that 7 June 1996 meeting, I awoke to the realization that if a loved one of mine committed murder, I would want the other cheek turned to them. And that I did not have the right to demand more from the world than I was willing to give to this man.

I have been on a long journey since seeing my father murdered. I have learned to let go. I have learned that vengeance is blinding and that while I may have the right to miss my father, I do not have the right to judge, condemn or hate who killed him. I have learned that while my life could never be the same after the murder, it didn't have to be worse. That was a matter of choice, my choice. And, I also learned that murder cannot destroy hope, faith or love.

www.annemariehagan.com

Camilla Carr and Jon James

Chechnya

I had learned from practising martial arts that to overcome your opponent you should meet hardness with softness.

In April 1997 Camilla Carr and her boyfriend, Jon James, went to Chechnya to set up a rehabilitation centre for traumatized war-children. Three months later they were taken hostage by Chechnyan rebels. Their ordeal lasted 14 months, during which Camilla was repeatedly raped by one of her jailers. Camilla and Jon have since written a memoir about their experiences, *The Sky is Always There*.

Camilla Carr

Rape is a terrible violation of a human being. I will never forgive the act, yet I can forgive the man who raped me; I can feel compassion for him because I understand the desperate place he was coming from.

That's not to say I condone what our captors did to us (the physical and psychological abuse was appalling), and if I met them now, I'd want to ask all of them, 'Did you have any idea how much you were harming us?' But I still understand the desperation that caused them to do the things they did.

As soon as we were taken hostage we decided to take the line of least resistance, because our four captors were so clearly traumatized by the war. If we'd shown anger or sadness, or resisted them in any way, we knew they could have reacted with violence.

After several weeks in captivity one of them – an ignorant and wounded person whom we named Paunch – took the opportunity to rape me. The only way I could get through this horror was by thinking to myself, 'You can never touch the essence of me – my body is only part of who I am.'

He raped me many times, but mostly I was able to cling on to a detached state of being. He always did it when he was alone and I didn't dare tell the other captors in case it gave them the idea of gang rape. This went on until I got herpes, which gave me the strength to resist. It didn't stop the sexual harassment completely until a month later. Jon and I were in the kitchen with Paunch and another of our captors, and Paunch went into another room and called me in. For the first time there was an open door and the others were there, which gave me the strength to kneel away from him and say, 'Niet, niet.' He looked surprised and asked me to get the dictionary. I pointed out, 'No sex, no violence.' He said, 'But you Western woman, free sex.' Then it was like a light switched on in his brain and I realized he wanted me as a friend. In his own way he was apologizing. He never touched me again after that but talked about his dreams of having a market garden and a four-wheel drive.

We were released in September 1998. Initially, I seemed to be doing well. We were basking in the euphoria of freedom and love from our family and friends. Then, two months later, I collapsed. I couldn't stop crying and had no energy. This lasted a few weeks, but it wasn't until 2001, when Jon and I moved to Wales, that I found the space and silence to let go and surrender to weakness and vulnerability. Only this way could my nervous system finally heal. Some of our Chechnyan friends can't understand how we can forgive. They feel tarnished with the guilt of their community. I tell them that I believe forgiveness begins with understanding, but you have to work through layers to obtain it. First you have to deal with anger, then with tears, and only once you reach the tears are you on the road to finding peace of mind.

Jon James

I had a horrible feeling as Paunch took Camilla next door. I heard a few muffled words, then silence, and an awful wave of realization hit me. I felt sick. I was powerless to take any physical action since I was handcuffed to the heating pipes. The only tool available was prayer. I prayed that the invasion would be swift and painless.

Throughout our ordeal, I continued to hold back my emotion, as I had learned from practising martial arts that to overcome your opponent you should meet hardness with softness. Knowing this saved my life. But in my dreams I murdered Paunch several times.

We'd do yoga and Tai Chi every morning and survived by the skin of our teeth. I got punched around and there was a lot of mental torture, even a mock execution at one point when we were certain we would die.

After our release we needed space. We'd been stuck together like glue for 14 months. We were both so used to supporting each other that we had to learn to stand alone again. For a long time I experienced anxiety and a lot of physical pain. Like Camilla, I've come to an understanding of where our captors, and where her violator, were coming from. Not many people in this world do stuff out of pure maliciousness. But it's taken me a long time to get to a point where I can think about what happened without feeling a charge of negative energy.

www.camillacarr.org

Jo Berry and Patrick Magee

Northern Ireland

Perhaps more than anything, I've realized that no matter which side of the conflict you're on, had we all lived each other's lives, we could all have done what the other did.

When Sir Anthony Berry MP was killed in the IRA Brighton Bombing during the 1984 Conservative Party Conference, his daughter Jo was thrown into a conflict she knew very little about. Since then she has visited Ireland many times and worked with victims and former combatants from all sides. In November 2000 she met Patrick Magee, the former IRA activist responsible for her father's death. Patrick had been given multiple life sentences for the Brighton Bombing but was released under the Good Friday Agreement in 1998. He has since been actively involved in peace work, including supporting Jo in her work with Building Bridges for Peace, a charity she founded to promote peace and better understand the roots of war, terrorism and violence.

Jo Berry

An inner shift is required to hear the story of the enemy. For me the question is always about whether I can let go of my need to blame, and open my heart enough to hear Patrick's story and understand his motivations. The truth is that sometimes I can and sometimes I can't. It's a journey and it's a choice, which means it's not all sorted and put away in a box.

It felt as if a part of me died in that bomb. I was totally out of my depth but somehow I held on to a small hope that something positive would come out of the trauma. So I went to Ireland and listened to the stories of many remarkable and courageous people who'd been caught up in the violence. For the first time I felt that my pain was being heard.

In those early years I probably used the word 'forgiveness' too liberally – I didn't really understand it. When I used the word on television, I was shocked to receive a death threat from a man who said I had betrayed both my father and my country.

Now I don't talk about forgiveness. To say 'I forgive you' is almost condescending – it locks you into an 'us and them' scenario, keeping me right and you wrong. That attitude won't change anything. But I can experience empathy, and in that moment there is no judgement. Sometimes when I've met with Patrick, I've had such a clear understanding of his life that there's nothing to forgive.

I wanted to meet Patrick to put a face to the enemy and see him as a real human being. At our first meeting I was terrified, but I wanted to acknowledge the courage it had taken him to meet me. We talked with an extraordinary intensity. I shared a lot about my father, while Patrick told me some of his story.

Over the past few years of getting to know Patrick, I feel I've been recovering some of the humanity I lost when that bomb went off. Patrick is also on a journey to recover his humanity. I know that he sometimes finds it hard to live with the knowledge that he cares for the daughter of someone he killed through his terrorist actions.

Perhaps more than anything, I've realized that no matter which side of the conflict you're on, had we all lived each other's lives, we could all have done what the other did. In other words, had I come from a Republican background, I could easily have made the same choices Patrick made.

Patrick Magee

Someday I may be able to forgive myself. Although I still stand by my actions, because at the time we were trapped and there was no other way, I will always carry the burden that I harmed other human beings. But I'm not seeking forgiveness. If Jo could just understand why someone like me could get involved in the armed struggle, then something has been achieved. The point is that Jo set out with that intent in mind – she wanted to know why.

I decided to meet Jo because, apart from addressing a personal obligation, I felt obligated as a Republican to explain what led someone like me to participate in the action. I told her that I'd got involved in the armed struggle at the age of 19, after witnessing how a small Nationalist community were being mistreated by the British. Those people had to respond. For 28 years I was active in the Republican movement. Even in jail I was still a volunteer.

Between Jo and me, the big issue is the use of violence. I can't claim to have renounced violence, though I don't believe I'm a violent person and have spoken out against it many times. I am 100 per cent in favour of the peace process, but I am not a pacifist and I could never say to future generations, anywhere in the world, who felt themselves oppressed, 'Take it, just lie down and take it.'

Jo told me that her daughter had said after one of our meetings, 'Does that mean that granddad Tony can come back now?' It stuck with me, because of course nothing has fundamentally changed. No matter what we can achieve as two human beings meeting after a terrible event, the loss remains and forgiveness can't embrace that loss. The hope lies in the fact that we are prepared to carry on. The dialogue has continued.

It's rare to meet someone as gracious and open as Jo. She's come a long way in her journey to understanding; in fact, she's come more than halfway to meet me. That's a very humbling experience.

www.buildingbridgesforpeace.org

Magdeline Makola

Scotland

Forgiveness is different from trusting. You don't have to trust someone just because they are forgiven.

In December 2008 Justice Ngema, an illegal immigrant from South Africa, abducted South African-born nurse Magdeline Makola from her home in Scotland, locking her in the boot of her car. It wasn't until ten days later that policemen heard Magdeline's muffled cries and rescued her. In 2009 Ngema received a minimum eight-year prison sentence.

Justice Ngema was a friend of an acquaintance of mine. He'd turned up at my door once before wanting to leave his bags in my flat, but I'd turned him away. I thought that was the end of it, but just before Christmas, late one night, he appeared again, this time wanting something to drink. I was very naive and let him in. A moment later he had grabbed me round the neck. 'I'm a professional at this job and I kill people if I want to,' he said, holding a knife to me. He pulled my arms around my back, held them with his knee, tied my hands and legs, then gagged and blindfolded me. Before I knew it, he'd dragged me over his shoulders and thrown me into my car. I was terrified.

We drove for hours. At one point he stopped at an ATM machine and cleared out my account. Then he demanded I get more money through telephone banking, but when that failed he started to get really angry. I was sure he meant to kill me.

But he didn't kill me. Instead, he just left me there all alone, trapped in the boot of my car with no idea where I was.

I lay there for hours, hating and despising him. I found this anger in me that I never knew I had. But when I realized he wasn't coming back, I knew I had to calm down. By now I had lost all track of time and was drifting in and out of consciousness. Occasionally I'd hear people talking and I'd try to call out but no one heard me. There was one very quiet day when I realized it was Christmas.

I prayed to God that someone would find me, but when no one came, I prepared myself for dying. I slept for long periods. I no longer felt anger or hatred – I wanted to die calmly. But just when I thought my life was over, I heard voices and somehow, chewing and struggling with the tape round my mouth, I was able to make a sound. 'Someone, please help me,' I cried feebly. This time, to my joy, I was heard.

I was rescued on Boxing Day, severely frostbitten, but alive! I was elated. It was the answer to all my prayers. My brother and my father soon came from South Africa to take care of me, and later I returned home to celebrate with my family. No one felt anger. We just thanked God that I had survived. My mother said she felt deep pity for Justice Ngema's mother.

Because of the joy of being found alive, I have never again felt any hatred towards Justice Ngema, but I have felt a deep sadness. We were both South Africans in a foreign country, and we should have helped one another, like brother and sister.

My recovery was remarkable. I didn't even suffer from post-traumatic stress. I think this is because I knew if I felt anger it would only delay my future and I'd end up suffering from depression. Some people think I'm crazy talking this way but I say, 'It's for my benefit and allows me to face life alone.'

The saddest thing of all for me is that after my ordeal some of my friends seemed more interested in talking to the media than in my well-being. With one close friend in particular, I have felt so betrayed and hurt. This did more damage than being locked in the boot of the car. I now have a problem with trust.

Before Ngema's trial I thought about visiting him to ask him why he did this to me, but because he showed no remorse at the trial and the authorities said he was still a danger to the public, I decided it was better to get on with my life and forget about him. Forgiveness is different from trusting. You don't have to trust someone just because they are forgiven.

It's hard to understand why he did what he did. He wasn't on drugs, he wasn't drunk and he didn't have mental problems. He was just a human being motivated by greed and desperation. My hope now is that in prison he comes into contact with people who can help him so that he can understand the harm that he did and change his life. You have to be positive to open up ways for someone to become a better person. If I hate him, I'll make him more entrenched in his attitude of greed and desperation. I want to give him a chance.

Samantha Lawler

USA

Forgiveness is not about forgiving the act but forgiving the imperfections which are inherent in all of us.

Samantha Lawler's mother was murdered by her father in 1999 at the family home in Fort Lauderdale, Florida. Her father admitted to strangling his wife, pleaded guilty to first-degree murder and rape, and was sentenced to life in prison without parole. Thirteen years later, Samantha visited her father in prison – an event which would change her life.

When my sister and I were old enough, my mum decided she didn't need to stay in an unhappy marriage any longer. When she told my dad she was planning to leave him, he didn't believe her and would say things like 'If you leave I'll put you six feet under.' But none of us believed him because that was the way he joked. He had never hurt or abused any of us – he just had this tough guy mentality.

It was a month before Christmas when it started getting really bad between my parents – constant fighting which made my mum certain she needed to leave him. We planned to leave after Christmas. Then one day I came home and my mum was lying on the couch. A friend came over and we stayed in my room for about an hour. When I came downstairs, I noticed my mum was in exactly the same position. I knew instantly then that something was terribly wrong. Rushing over to her, I saw her face was covered in blue spots and it was obvious she was dead. When I saw her purse lying next to her, I realized it wasn't a burglar who had done this – it had to be my dad.

The paramedics arrived, my mum's body was carried out in a body bag and I realized at that point that nothing would ever be the same again. It was like someone had shut the door and turned off the light.

For the next 13 years I didn't have a good view of the world. My life was a muted, drunken blur. If people complained they had bad relationships with their family, I had no tolerance whatsoever. I was consumed by a potent mix of grief and anger – grief that I'd lost my mum and anger with my dad for taking her away.

I grieved, but because my parents had both been such amazing people, who had instilled in me ways of coping, I was able to function. I went out, had relationships and appeared to be my normal self. People would tell me it was good to cry, so sometimes I would spend a whole afternoon crying – but it didn't help. As the years passed, it made no difference to the level of grief and hopelessness I felt.

Finally, when I was 32, I took a three-day personal development workshop. There were a hundred people in the group and I could see how we all shared similar stories of fear, anger, jealousy and despair. What I took from that course was a strong feeling of empathy and compassion towards humanity. I felt empowered and tried to practise what I'd learnt in my everyday life by calling up people from my past to set things right. As I made a list of all the people I'd turned my back on, I finally came across my dad. I really was not expecting to work on that part of my life, but I realized now that my dad must also be dealing with anger, loss and frustration.

I immediately contacted the facility where he was incarcerated and found out they had been trying to get hold of me because my father was in a critical condition, quite literally on his death bed. And so, in October 2012, I set out from New York to Florida to visit him.

I was only given ten minutes with my father. He was unrecognizable, a shell of his former self. He'd had multiple strokes and his muscles had atrophied. He was breathing from a tube, couldn't talk and was handcuffed to the bed. He also had AIDS. But his eyes were open and for all those ten minutes he made eye contact with me.

I was overwhelmed. So this was what judgement looked like! Suddenly I realized he was doing what I'd always wanted – suffering terribly. The shock and the appalling state he was in cleaned the slate clean for me. I told him over and over how much I loved him and that I forgave him. And I apologized for waiting so long to come to see him and to tell him this. I realized later that during those ten minutes there were no feelings of hate or guilt, or right and wrong. There was just a deep connection. No conservation was necessary, no apology. For ten minutes I got my dad back and when I left I felt this incredible weight drop away.

I still can hardly believe how the very thing I didn't want to do – see my dad again – is exactly what has given me my life back. I still miss my mum just as much, but it's as if that whole dark part of how she died isn't there anymore. And I have compassion for my dad now in the way that you have compassion for the bully who uses aggression to mask pain and hurt.

Also, forgiveness for me is absolute and final. There isn't a day I wonder whether I have forgiven my father or not. I've come to believe that we all have good and bad in us; we're all figuring life out as best we can. When people make the wrong choices, they are figuring it out too. Forgiveness is not about forgiving the act but forgiving the imperfections which are inherent in all of us.

Martin Snodden

Northern Ireland

I have had to seek forgiveness within myself in order to reconcile my past and present.

As a former paramilitary, Martin Snodden has served a life sentence in the Maze Prison for his activities as a member of the Ulster Volunteer Force (UVF). Fifteen years later he was released under licence. He now operates as an independent international trainer and consultant.

What drove me to take up arms was a desire for peace. Violence was visited upon me in 1969 when I was 15 years old. I lived in a Catholic Nationalist area of West Belfast, part of a small Protestant community that came under attack on a daily basis. So-called freedom fighters were denying my family, my neighbours and my friends the right to live in peace. State forces, the police and army weren't present, so it was a question of self-defence.

Between the ages of 16 and 19 I actively engaged in violence, and before I had turned 20 I was imprisoned for my actions – in particular, for an attack on a premises that was a base for an IRA unit. Two people lost their lives in that attack. One was my colleague and comrade, who died when a bomb prematurely exploded. The other was a woman, an innocent civilian, who was on the premises at the time. My comrades in prison were like me; most had entered prison before the age of 22. All were cannon fodder.

While I was incarcerated I had the opportunity to explore Irish history, and to ask why, despite my Christian upbringing, and despite my strong belief in a moral existence, I had contributed to the violence of our political conflict. I have since come to the conclusion that these beliefs can co-exist: that respect for a moral/ spiritual authority can live alongside the need to act to defend one's community.

My personal inner journey was long and tortuous, but I grew to believe that violence was not going to resolve our political conflict, or repair our damaged and divided communities. So while in prison I sat down and spoke with some of my enemies. I developed a very strong friendship with one particular Republican prisoner – a friendship that was not to everyone's liking.

In 1990 I was released under licence. The authorities expected prisoners like me to reintegrate back into society, but upon release I found that this was not a society I wanted to reintegrate with. The polarization had only increased, and my moderate views were now as marginalized as my extremist views had been prior to my incarceration. Nevertheless, I still desired change in our society, and this time I resolved to do it through relationship building and conflict resolution.

This is the path I've been walking ever since – sometimes with extreme difficulty. I have to always consider my family and the risks I'm taking. In the past I received death threats from both sides. The work I engage in can be very challenging for some people. It would have been so much easier to have taken a job in industry and just become insignificant in our society.

In my life I've been a peace breaker, a peacemaker and peace builder. My past violent actions were very destructive, but now I'm fighting for peace in a far more constructive manner. The risks aren't really much different but the rewards are much greater.

The Conflict Trauma Resource Centre project, which I was instrumental in developing and leading for 12 years, contributed to addressing the trauma, pain and suffering legacy of our violent conflict. People who use violence are likely not only to kill someone else but also to kill part of themselves in the course of those violent actions. They lose part of their humanity. I deeply regret how my violent actions hurt innocent people. I have had to seek forgiveness within myself and to reconcile my past and my present. That in itself has put me in a better place and empowered me to address the needs of others with regard to the legacy of the violent conflict.

Katy Hutchison and Ryan Aldridge

Canada

Part of being human is rolling up our sleeves and taking an active part in repairing harm.

On New Year's Eve 1997 Katy Hutchison's husband, Bob, was beaten to death while checking on a party being thrown by his neighbour's son. In the small town of Squamish in British Columbia, a wall of silence soon grew up around the murder. It was four years before Ryan Aldridge admitted to having delivered the fatal blow. He was convicted of manslaughter and sentenced to five years in prison. Ryan has since been released from prison. He is employed and happily married with one child. In 2006 Katy wrote the book *Walking After Midnight: One Woman's Journey Through Murder, Justice, and Forgiveness*.

Katy Hutchison

Less than an hour after Bob was murdered, I stood in the emergency ward beside his body, overwhelmed by a sense of peace, knowing that wherever Bob was now, it was much safer than the place he had just been. Then I went home to tell my four-year-old twins, Amelia and Sam, that their daddy was dead. I looked into their eyes and knew that I could not allow their lives to become dominated by their father's death. I promised them and I promised myself that underneath the horror of what had just happened we would find a gift.

As for the rest of the community, the code of silence began that night. No one called the police, no one spoke out. The murder was devastating, but the silence from so many compounded the devastation. In the end, I chose to leave my community and return to the community I had grown up in.

Eventually, after four years, Ryan Aldridge was arrested. That same day, as I was leaving the police station, I spotted him on camera, alone in the investigation room. The police had left the tape rolling and I stood and watched him falling apart. I didn't want to leave him. He was someone's child.

After his arrest, police officers showed Ryan a video I'd made for him, urging him to dig down deep to find the words to say, 'I did this.' Four years of silence, grief and fear then fell away as he fulfilled my wish and confessed to the crime. Those words would begin the healing process for both of us. He then stunned police by asking to meet me, and so, less than 24 hours after his arrest, I found myself face-to-face with the man who had murdered my husband. As he sobbed, it was all I could do not to hold him. Second to the day I gave birth, it was probably the most human moment of my life.

Sometime into Ryan's sentence I discovered an incredible organization called Community Justice Initiatives that was able to organize a victim–offender reconciliation between Ryan and me. It took place in the prison and lasted most of the day: we spoke about almost everything – our lives, our hobbies, our families.

There were tears, there were long silences where neither of us had the words to fill the space. In that meeting I told Ryan that I had forgiven him.

I've been able to forgive Ryan because of the immense sympathy I have for his mother. I understood her loss. We haven't met yet but we write and I cherish her letters. Forgiveness isn't easy. Taking tranquillizers and having someone look after your kids would probably be easier, but I feel compelled to do something with Bob's legacy. I want to tell my story to help change people's perceptions – and where possible I want to do this with Ryan by my side. I'll never understand how our universes collided – but they did, and if Bob can't make further contribution to society, then perhaps Ryan can. Whether victim or perpetrator, part of being human is rolling up our sleeves and taking an active part in repairing harm.

Amelia and Sam supported my choice to forgive Ryan, but others have asked, 'How could you?' The way I saw it, how could I not? My children had lost their father and I did not want them to lose me in the process. If I had been consumed by hatred, anger and vengeance, what kind of mother would I be? Something happened when Bob died and I found my voice. Forgiveness became an opportunity to create a new and hopeful beginning.

Looking back 17 years, I realize how dynamic the forgiveness experience has been. It changes shape; some days growing, others withering. It is heart work of the highest order. I am thankful to Ryan for making the very best of his life, moving forward and working hard to care for his family and contribute to his community. But mostly I remain grateful for the brave hearts of my now-adult children and my second husband Michael, who supported my choice and trusted me on this uncharted journey of the heart.

Ryan Aldridge

Katy's forgiveness is the most incredible thing that anyone has ever given me. It changed my life. There's trouble every day in prison, offers of drugs and threats of fights, but I didn't give in. My life would still be full of anger and violence if it wasn't for Katy.

I grew up in a small town. I was bullied as a child but eventually I started hanging around with a group whose lifestyle impressed me. For the first time I felt accepted. By the age of 16 we were experimenting with drink and drugs and the partying began.

Unfortunately, I started getting into trouble with the local police and was involved in three separate alcohol-related car crashes. Separate to this, a good friend then died in a car accident which totally devastated me.

On New Year's Eve 1997, a friend was throwing a party. His father was away. There were over 150 guests, and with so much alcohol and drugs going around fights started breaking out. When a stranger came up the stairs and asked us all to leave, my friend hit him. He fell to the ground and I kicked him four times in the head. After that I moved on to another party, not knowing I'd made the worst mistake of my life.

Throughout the investigation, the secret of my crime began to destroy me. I became depressed and introverted. I could well have committed suicide if, after four years, I hadn't broken my silence. My family was devastated.

Having admitted my guilt, I wanted to apologize face-to-face for what had happened. So, within an hour of being arrested, I wrote a letter to Katy and her children, apologizing for what I'd done. I also asked a police officer if I could meet with her. I'd read about Katy in the papers but never expected her forgiveness. If I put myself in her shoes, I think I would have hated the person who had done what I'd done to her.

The big question I still ask myself is 'Why did you do this?' And I still can't find an answer. Doing time is easy compared with the guilt I'll have to live with for the rest of my life. But with Katy's forgiveness, I hope that perhaps, one day, I'll be able to forgive myself.

www.katyhutchisonpresents.com

Gill Hicks

England

My commitment is to understand why a 19-year-old man from the north of England would take his own life and want to take mine.

On 7 July 2005, 52 people died and many more were severely injured and maimed by suicide bombers attacking London's transport system. On a Piccadilly line underground train, between King's Cross and Russell Square stations, Australian-born Gill Hicks miraculously survived but lost both her legs in the explosion. Gill's memoir, *One Unknown*, was published in 2008.

As I lay waiting – trapped in what resembled a train carriage but was now a blackened, smoke-filled indescribable 'room' of destruction and devastation – I was able to think. This period of time, some 60 minutes, was to prove to be the most insightful and blessed gift of time that I am yet to receive, apart, that is, from the ultimate gift of a second chance at life.

Incredibly, I believe I was offered the choice of Life. As the blood poured from my body (despite the scarf I had tied on each leg as a tourniquet to stem the flow), I felt weak, fighting to hold on, to survive.

There were two voices holding a very powerful but conflicting conversation in my head – one 'voice' willing me to hold on, telling me that there was so much to achieve, how my life could make a positive difference. The other 'voice' was calling me softly, telling me that it was all right to let go, to drift away into a deep, peaceful and permanent sleep. Both sides were stating their case – asking me to choose between life and death.

I wanted to live. I wanted to survive and so I chose Life. Once I made this decision the conversation ended. I wasn't going to die in the carriage, not down there in that tunnel and not on that day.

Within an hour, help arrived by way of the emergency services. Each person who 'saved' me that day did so without knowing who I was. To them, it didn't matter if I was rich or poor, black or white, female or male, Muslim or Jew, religious or not. What mattered to the police, the paramedics, the surgeons, the nurses and all who never gave up the effort to save my life was that I was a precious human being. I arrived at hospital labelled as 'One Unknown' – an estimated female.

When I awoke, I was euphoric to be alive and to have survived. I felt like a very blessed person – filled with emotions of love and compassion, empathy and joy. I promised myself that if I survived the bomb blast, I would honour the gift of life by doing all I could to give back, to make a greater contribution to the world and to live it to the fullest.

And honouring Life is to live without hatred, to not seek revenge or want violent retribution; to ensure that the cycle of conflict ends with me. I don't see these actions or feelings as forgiveness, as I question if the suicide bomber would want my forgiveness, and he is dead, so we shall never know. All I can do is follow the example so brilliantly shown to me by all those who saved my life – that humanity, empathy, compassion are the attributes that I want to take into my second chance, my life number 2. My commitment is to be on the journey of understanding, to understand why a 19-year-old man from the north of England would take his own life and want to take mine.

I knew instinctively that the vow I made in the carriage to make a difference was exactly what I needed to do, so I left my career within architecture and design and created a not-for-profit business, called Making a Difference for Peace or M.A.D. My focus was to do all I could to deter anyone from falling under the influence of destructive extremist ideas and, worse, becoming human weapons.

Through my experience and the sharing of my story, my work has helped create an alternative narrative, that we are all interconnected and interdependent, each and every 'One Unknown'; it is not 'us' and 'them'.

I am the legacy of all those who never gave up trying to save my life, and in January 2013 I went on to create my own legacy – I gave birth to a beautiful daughter, Amelie. There hasn't been a single day since that fateful morning on 7 July 2005 when I have not been grateful to have my life, and there has not been a single moment since having my daughter that I have not been in awe of the wonder of life, that my life has gone on to create a new life. Amelie has it all ahead of her, to make her choices and decisions. All that I hope to instil is that she makes a positive contribution and a great difference in anything she does.

Tomorrow is for Amelie and all our children, but Today is for us all to build the strong foundations on which Tomorrow will stand. Building a sustainable peace is, I believe, our collective responsibility. I would like to raise my child in a world whose people were empathetic and actively engaged in peace as part of their everyday. I would like to live and share in a world where the killing and maiming of innocent people is not a course of action, is no longer a reality. I would like to live in a world whose people were M.A.D.

www.madminds.org
www.bethebridge.co

TJ Leyden
USA

I used to think people were showing me respect, until eventually I came to realize that the only reason they were showing me respect was because they feared me.

In 1980, at the age of 14, TJ Leyden became a neo-Nazi skinhead, soon rising through the ranks of Hammerskin Nation, the largest white supremacist transnational organization in America. After 15 years of spreading hate, bigotry and racism, TJ turned his back on the white power movement. He has since worked with the Task Force Against Hate at the Simon Wiesenthal Center in Los Angles and is the author of *Skinhead Confessions: From Hate to Hope*.

Coming from an Irish Catholic home, I was taught that boys don't cry, men rule and women are second-class citizens. So when my mother tried to talk me out of getting involved in the white power movement, I wouldn't listen to her.

Later I joined the US military where I started recruiting. I developed strong bonds with gang members inside the military and when I left I joined the largest neo-Nazi skinhead organization in the country as a street solider. At first I didn't really like the violence but after a while it didn't bother me one bit; it was just something we did. I wouldn't even be able to tell you how many victims I had.

The gang gave me everything I lacked – identity, purpose, a direction in life. I felt a complete sense of right because I was preserving my identity and my culture. We felt under attack from blacks, from Latinos and from multiculturalism in general. We set the rules and there was no room for dissent: dialogue was a sign of weakness. In the early 90s I married a girl in the white supremacy movement. I figured I was in love, and since we were both so good at hating, why not raise kids to hate like us! My first kid was two days old when I first went to prison and for the next ten years I was in and out of jail.

When the change finally came, it was a series of epiphanies. The first epiphany happened when I was watching a Caribbean-style children's show with my sons, and my younger son – then aged three – suddenly just switched off the TV, announcing, 'Daddy! We don't watch Niggers!' At first I felt proud that he was turning into a racist like me, but then I started thinking...if I wasn't raised to be a racist and I had turned out the way I was, then how much worse would my children be! And then it hit me – if I didn't want my sons to grow up to be like me, there must be something fundamentally wrong with the whole premise and purpose of my life.

Slowly I began to think beyond the black-and-white rhetoric of my group. I began to imagine what might happen if the whole world was white. Would we then be saying, 'We're going to get rid of all non-racist pagans,' or, 'Everyone with a genetic defect is the next to go'? Finally it got to a point where I had to choose which path of life I was going to take.

When I decided to get out of the movement, I went first to my mother's house to apologize for everything I'd put her through. The next morning she suggested I went to the Simon Wiesenthal Museum of Tolerance in LA, to apologize to them. I thought she was crazy but she was so persuasive. So I rang them and said, 'My name is TJ. I've got all this racist literature and material and I want to hand it over to you.' They were flabbergasted but invited me along. I learnt later that I was the first neo-Nazi to voluntarily and publicly give up the movement and hand over racist material and evidence.

At that first meeting the rabbi was hesitant, but ten days later he invited me back. I was asked if I'd speak out about my friends in the white power movement and I agreed. What was amazing was that for the first time in my life here was a group of individuals who honestly believed I could do good in the world. For the first time I experienced real compassion. In fact, the greatest compassion I've ever experienced is when I spoke at a synagogue and a Jewish Holocaust survivor came up to me and said they forgave me.

The easiest thing for me was to give up racism, because it's an 'ism' and people change isms all the time. The harder thing was to give up my sense of power, entitlement and privilege. I used to think people were showing me respect, until eventually I came to realize that the only reason they were showing me respect was because they feared me.

These days I receive death threats all the time, and there are websites on the internet targeting me. People ask if I hate these people who would like to see me dead, but I say, 'No, I feel empathy and compassion for them because they've not yet seen the light that I've seen.' I find I'm able to carry their hate.

Geoff Thompson

England

Forgiveness is pragmatic. It offers a real and lasting vengeance.

Geoff Thompson grew up in working-class Coventry. At the age of 12 he was abused by an adult he trusted. The incident shattered his self-esteem and led to a decade of violence. He has since become a martial arts instructor, teacher and author of more than 34 books. The short film *Romans 12:20* tells Geoff's story and his autobiographical play *Fragile* examines the cause and effect of trauma in forensic detail.

My lovely mum always said that I inherited her nerves. Certainly I was a sensitive kid, and felt the lash of depression from an early age. My first encounter with it was when I moved to senior school. The transition overwhelmed me and I felt threatened at every corner. In a bid to win some courage I started training in martial arts.

My martial arts instructor was a charismatic man who took me under his wing. I was in awe of him and, after a short period of subtle and insidious grooming, he asked me and some of the other boys to stay over at the club to help fix the aikido mats. That night I awoke to the feeling of a hand on my bare leg. The level of the sexual abuse that followed was not extreme – I was not raped – but the level of betrayal proved to be catastrophic. Most of that night is lost to my memory but I remember waking up the next morning knowing my childhood had ended.

I have visited this place in my mind many times since but those hours still remain lost. All I remember was waking up the next day with the darkest depression squatting deep inside my breast. For a long time I didn't tell anyone – especially not my mum. She had always warned us never to bring shame to her door, and I had made it my raison d'être never to cause her pain.

What this abuser taught me implicitly with his actions was that no one could be trusted, not even those who loved you. This, of course, had a detrimental effect on my malleable mind. An incident that puts you out by a small degree as a 12-year-old is enough to send you completely off the grid by the time you're 30. At 14, I was kissing a girl in the farmer's field and her face contorted into the face of a man. At 15 (and for many years after) I had uncontrollable and unwelcome fantasies about the abuse. This triggered a lot of guilt and shame in me. It was only many years later, after studying psychology, that I understood this was my mind's way of trying to gain some sort of control over my angst by re-imagining the abuse as a pleasurable experience. As an adult, I developed psychotic jealousy, imagining that every girl I dated was cheating on me.

At 28, I became a nightclub bouncer in a bid to mould myself a bit of spine. I was a man with a lot of underlying rage and I displaced my anger on anyone that stepped into my orbit. It took a decade of extreme violence before I realized that I was out of control. When I nearly killed a man in a car park match fight, I knew it was time to leave. I wrote a book about my exploits, left the doors and renounced violence.

During my violent days, I thought forgiveness was weak and meant letting people off the hook. That changed when I started teaching forgiveness to my martial arts students. Even though I understood forgiveness intellectually, I didn't understand it in practice until, one day, I was sitting in a café and saw my abuser sitting at the table opposite. For a split second I was 12 again, quivering with fear.

But then I walked over to him. I introduced myself and told him what he had done to me as a child and how it had affected me. He was a big man, and he tried to stand up and protest. I put my hand out and told him to sit down. He obeyed immediately. I told him that despite what he had done I was going to forgive him. I told him twice. He looked totally broken. It was as if my forgiveness shattered him. As I went to walk away, he put his hand out. I hesitated. I wanted to be free from this man's memory and I knew that the only way to be free was to properly forgive him. So I shook his trembling hand. When I walked away from that café, I felt the most powerful man in the world. I had taken all my power back from him.

Years later I heard that he'd committed suicide. His past caught up with him; the police were finally on his trail after 30 years. There was no celebration from me. I felt only sadness. There could be no justifying his heinous crimes but I had a lot of compassion for him. He was a man with potential, and he wasted his life.

I came to realize that if someone abused me 20 years ago and I did not forgive them, they were still abusing me now, today; in fact, they were literally holding me in stasis. Forgiveness not only gives you power over the here-and-now and over the future, it also deems you impervious to your past. It literally allows you to dismantle historical trauma.

Post the Jimmy Saville affair, people are understandably suspicious, even angry, when you talk about forgiveness in connection with a paedophile: did I really forgive my abuser, or did I just let him off, and in doing so indirectly condone his actions and leave the way open for further abuse? The nature of such enquiries is unkind, and the subtext is loaded with judgement and implication. This is the dangerous naivety and presumption of the observer who sees only two options in sex-related abuse: a day in court or a violent revenge. Forgiveness is not even in their lexicon; they fail to see its potency. When you have tried and been failed by the judiciary and blood-lust turns you into a monster, what are you left with? Forgiveness is pragmatic. It offers a real and lasting vengeance.

www.geoffthompson.com

Grace Idowu

England

When I recovered myself, I told him, 'I'm not crying for David, I'm crying for you. What have you done with your life?'

In 2008 Tim and Grace Idowu's third child, 14-year-old David, was murdered in the park opposite his home in South London. The perpetrator was 16-year-old Elijah Dayoni who later received a minimum sentence of 12 years. In 2010 Grace met Elijah at a restorative justice victim-offender meeting at Ashfield Young Offenders Institute. The David Idowu Foundation has been set up by Grace and Tim in memory of their son to educate young people about the dangers of gun and knife crime.

It was a warm day in June and I was working behind the till at Tesco's when two police officers came through the door. At first I thought they were after a shoplifter but then they asked me to come to the manager's office with them. 'We're here to tell you that one of your boys has been stabbed,' they said. I don't remember what happened next but I woke up on the floor. Then I heard someone say, 'Grace, he isn't dead.' When they told me it was David who had been stabbed, I was so shocked, and I knew then that whoever stabbed David could not have known him.

By the time I arrived at the hospital I was on fire and couldn't stop shaking. 'We've resuscitated him twice already,' the doctor said. My youngest son, James, was then brought to me, and later my husband arrived. On hearing the news he just collapsed, rolling on the floor, crying like a baby. Our James tried to pull him up, saying to his father, 'You've forgotten what you always say; you say that we should pray.'

I'd never seen my husband cry before and when I saw my little boy so confused I knew I couldn't let what was happening to David break our family apart. I knew I had to stay strong. And so we started praying. Those hours were like a thousand years. We walked up and down, crying and praying.

We were there for 20 days and every day they were working on David. He lost 90 per cent of his blood as they tried to stitch his heart together. After ten days they had to amputate one of his legs to save his life. Then his liver packed up. The doctors tried their best but on the 19th day we were told his second leg would also have to be removed. That was the hardest. And then, on the 20th day, David passed away.

Three days after David was attacked the police had come to tell me they'd caught the boy who stabbed him. I told them I didn't want to know anything about Elijah until they investigated David. I knew he wasn't involved in crime, but I also knew if I said wonderful things about my son they'd just think it was a mother protecting her child. So I was satisfied when three months later the police returned and said they'd spoken to lots of people and couldn't pin a single thing on David. Even the dinner ladies at his school cried when they heard what had happened.

Throughout the trial Elijah didn't say anything, but on the day he was sentenced he wrote a letter, which was passed from his barrister to the judge. In it he said that he was very sorry.

In the months that followed we took everything to God to try to make peace with what had happened. But my husband was still very angry and James became increasingly withdrawn. He and David had done everything together. I thought about David all the time, but I also thought about this boy Elijah and after a while I told the police I wanted to meet him. In 2009 the police asked Elijah but he refused to see me. I asked them to try again and the following year he agreed. My husband didn't want to come. He said, 'I don't want to risk doing something nasty to this boy.'

When I arrived in the room, Elijah was crying bitterly with his head held low. I'd been told he'd been crying all morning and the officer had told him the meeting could still be cancelled, but he'd insisted on going ahead.

The priest from the prison and a police officer were with us. I asked to sit next to Elijah, but they said I had to sit opposite him with a table between us. I said to the officer, 'I'm not strong enough to strangle him, you know.'

The first thing I asked Elijah was 'Did you know David?' He said, 'No.' I then asked, 'So why?' Elijah said, 'I stabbed him because he was from a rival school and I had a knife.' That was when I broke down; it was the first time I'd cried in front of other people. When I recovered myself, I told him, 'I'm not crying for David, I'm crying for you. What have you done with your life?' Then he said, 'Please, Grace, don't hate me. I didn't mean to kill your boy.'

I told him about David and about David's three brothers. I said, 'You've taken our best friend from us.' And then I leaned over and said, 'But I want you to know that I forgive you,' and I hugged him.

I left that day feeling a huge sense of relief not only for me but also because one day this young man will be released from prison and I don't want his bitterness to destroy his life as well as the lives of others.

I also asked Elijah to write a letter to David's three brothers, which he later did. This gave them back their strength and confidence. Then last year my husband, who had been so angry, told me that through prayer he had found it in his heart to forgive Elijah. 'I too could now sit in the same room with him,' he said.

www.davididowufoundation.com

Jude Whyte

Northern Ireland

*Most people
won't ever forgive
because they see
it as stampeding
on the memory of
their loved ones.*

Jude Whyte was born in Belfast in 1957 to Catholic parents. After the sectarian conflict started in the late 1960s, several of his seven siblings left for England but Jude remained in Belfast, taking a Sociology degree and getting married. In April 1984 his life changed forever when his mother, a part-time taxi driver, was killed in a bomb blast outside the family home.

I had no real inkling that I lived in an abnormal society until the student civil rights protests started at the end of our road in the 1960s. My mother used to say they were all trouble makers. Even though she was Catholic, she was a fan of the British state which had brought her 'child benefit' and free education. In no way were we a hotbed of radicals. In fact, every night after dinner we'd turn the telly off, get down on our knees and say the rosary.

In 1969 the violence escalated and before we knew it people were dying and Belfast imploded in sectarian violence. When internment was introduced and people – mostly Catholics – were detained without trial, there was virtually a civil war.

By the time I went to grammar school, every afternoon after school I'd put my bag behind a bin and go and fight the British Army with bricks and bottles. It became a normal part of growing up. The fear started when I saw a young fellow die next to me, hit by a battery fired from a gun. Then on 5 September 1971 a member of the UDR (the legal regiment of the British army) stopped me in the street to ask what my father's name was. When I told him, he said he was going to kill my father because he was obviously a *fenian* (a derogatory term for a Catholic). I asked why and he said, 'Because we hate *fenians*.' They saw me, in my school uniform, as the enemy. That was the day my childhood ended.

The first time our home was bombed was in 1983 by a young Ulster Volunteer Force (UVF) man who lived a mile away. When he blew himself up, it was my mother who comforted him and told me to get a pillow for under his head. If I've ever seen a victim in my life, it was him. He was alone and cold with only my mother to help him.

A part of me thought the UVF wouldn't come back because we'd saved this man's life, but they did and this time they made no mistake. When my mother spotted the bomb on the window ledge outside the sitting room, she called the police. Unfortunately, it exploded as she was opening the door, killing both her and the young police officer, Michael Dawson, who'd come to investigate.

The police were basically our enemy but my mother had taught me to reach out to those in need and one of the first things I did was go to the house of the young police officer to offer our condolences. It was the beginning of the journey I'm now on.

In those days there was no counselling or trauma advice, and initially I was full of bile and hatred. I was a bad father, a bad husband and a bad lecturer. My thoughts were only of revenge and

I could feel the bitterness eating me up. Eventually I had a nervous breakdown and knew I had to change.

Forgiveness was for me both a pragmatic decision and an emotional feeling – it had nothing to do with religion. It meant that I lived a lot easier, I slept a lot better. You could say my revenge for the murder of my mother is my forgiveness because it has given me strength. I don't forgive on behalf of my mother but for the pain that was inflicted on me for the loss of my mother. And while my mother may not have given me permission to forgive, she did tell me to get a pillow for the UVF man who tried to blow us up.

Although there is very little forgiveness in Northern Ireland, we have made remarkable progress. We are still a toxic society but we are not a violent society. However, people like me are part of the problem. I was never a member of the IRA and I never held a gun, but still when Protestants were killed I stood by. Because I only protested when my own community were hurt, I'm as guilty as those who committed acts of violence.

I believe the only way to reconcile is to get to the truth and the only way we can do that is if we have a general amnesty for everyone on both sides. It would mean no one going to prison for what they did in the past. This would create the conditions for accountability where people feel safe enough to talk. I know that many people want the perpetrators to go to jail, but the trouble is, even if they are convicted, under the Good Friday Agreement the maximum sentence they would ever serve is just two years.

I still know a lot of people for whom the totality of their existence is the events that happened several decades ago. Many are still broken and most people won't ever forgive because they see it as stampeding on the memory of their loved ones.

Wilma Derksen

Canada

We knew that murder takes a life but we also knew that the aftermath of murder can be just as deadly.

In November 1984 Wilma and Cliff Derksen's 13-year-old daughter, Candace, went missing on her way home from school in Winnipeg, Canada. It wasn't until 22 years later that Mark Grant was charged with her murder and, in 2011, after a five-week trial, sentenced to 25 years without parole. For the past three decades Wilma has influenced victims, offenders and her local community by writing and speaking on the subject of forgiveness.

For six and a half weeks we didn't know what had happened to Candace. She just disappeared into thin air. But everyone knows that when a 13-year-old girl goes missing, then something is terribly wrong. She was a child in a woman's body, that moment of vulnerability when one minute they're a child and the next a woman.

Eventually Candace's body was found in a shack not far from our home – her hands and feet had been tied. Someone had forced her there but we lived with the mystery of not knowing who had done this for the next 22 years.

The day her body was found, all our friends came to visit, bringing warm food with them. There was so much love in the house that it helped us get through. Then at around 10.30 that evening, when most people had left, there was a knock on the door and this stranger stood there. He told us, 'I'm the parent of a murdered child too.' He was saying we now belonged to an exclusive club that no one wants to belong to. We invited him to the kitchen table and for the next two hours he told us in vivid detail everything he'd lost – his health, his relationships, his concentration, his ability to work. He'd even lost all memory of his daughter because now he could only think of the murder, the trauma and the hate that followed.

Cliff and I went to bed that night horrified by the graphic picture he'd painted. Having just been through the pain of losing our daughter, it now seemed we might lose everything else as well. And so we made a decision that night that we would respond differently, and we chose the path of forgiveness.

This decision was validated and verified the next day at the press conference when a reporter asked us what we thought of the offender, and we replied that our intention was to forgive. From then on we became known as the couple who had forgiven. In hindsight, I don't think we had any idea what forgiveness looked like in the face of murder, but our state of mind at the time was such that we knew we had to say no to anger and obsession. We determined to resist anything that would keep us in a state of emotional bondage, both for our sake and the sake of our other two children.

Little did I know that the word 'forgiveness' would haunt me for the next 30 years – prod me, guide me, heal me, label me, enlighten me, imprison me, free me and, in the end, define me. I was right out there in public – confessing to everyone the desire of my heart. When I joined Family Survivors of Homicide, I was quite forcibly told to forget about using the word 'forgiveness' because they could only see the dangers of forgiving. In some ways that was good for me because, as a Mennonite, it made me lose the religious lingo and forced me to be more authentic. Forgiveness is a hard word, it demands a lot of you and is so often misunderstood.

At times it was incredibly tough. People said we couldn't have loved Candace because we forgave. One woman said my stance was dangerous because I was promoting a society where all the murderers would go free. Also, because the perpetrator hadn't been found, some people were suspicious of Cliff.

But it's true that your enemy becomes your best and most wonderful teacher because people's reactions taught us who our friends really were. You can't play games around murder – there's a kind of vulnerability and transparency that occurs and you have to become a better person to get through. You can't stay around in the fog. You need to soar, to go higher. That's forgiveness.

Not knowing who the killer was for all those years didn't stop us from moving forward but we had to fight against becoming obsessed. We knew that murder takes a life but we also knew – through the appearance of the bereaved father at our door – that the aftermath of murder can be just as deadly.

Then, in 2007, everything charged when Mark Grant was charged with Candace's murder. We'd come to grips with living with the unknown and now we were right back at the beginning with all the old emotions of fear, anger and grief. At one point I got very sick; my whole body ached and I knew it was the anger.

When Mark Grant received 25 years without parole, his sentence seemed to match the gravity of the offence and we were satisfied. But unfortunately that wasn't the end of it because since then the case has gone to appeal and is currently before Canada's top court. It's troubling to think we might have to go through another trial, the waste of public money and the ongoing 'guilty or not guilty' debate that erodes the public's faith in the justice system. However, we as a family are content to go on with our lives and leave it with the attorneys now. We are just continually grateful that there was a trial and our justice system did come through for us in revealing the true story.

For me, forgiving has been about turning what has happened to us into good. Forgiveness is not just a one-off event, nor does it mean you're doing the same thing again and again. The issues of Candace's murder present themselves differently every day. Forgiveness is a fresh, ongoing, ever-present position of the mind which takes on many different forms. It's a promise of what we want to do, a goal, a North Star, a mantra.

www.wilmaderksen.com

Satta Joe

Sierra Leone

As I took his hand I was sobbing – not out of despair but a sense of relief that perhaps now we could move on from this terrible pain in our past.

Satta Joe was a victim of the Sierra Leone Civil War (1991–2002). She lives in the Kono District – an area with rich diamond reserves which experienced devastation during the war when looting and constant fighting took place between the RUF (Revolutionary United Front) rebels and Government forces. The war left more than 50,000 people dead and over two million people displaced in neighbouring countries. The organization Fambul Tok (Family Talk) emerged as a unique approach to community reconciliation in post-conflict Sierra Leone and has helped rebuild many lives, including that of Satta Joe.

I was in my third trimester of pregnancy when we started hearing news that the rebels were advancing towards our village. By the time they finally captured it, I had just given birth. Most of my family members escaped and hid in the surrounding bush, but I couldn't run so my husband stayed behind to be by my side.

When the rebels entered my village, there was one person I recognized among them and that was my own blood relative – Nyuma Saffa. He was now the leader of this particular band of rebels and was the first to enter my house. I was shocked when I saw him and screamed out of fear because he had previously tried to force me into loving him. When he saw me, he looked at me and said, 'I failed to convince you to fall in love with me before, so now that I've caught up with you and you're at my mercy, I'm going to do with you as I please.' Then he announced that he was going to rape me. I pleaded with him not to do this as I was a feeding mother, but he took no notice and went on to rape me several times. Afterwards some more rebels came and they all took turns to rape me. When my husband saw this, he panicked and, fearing for his own life, ran away, leaving me behind. Unfortunately for him, on his way out of the village, he met another band of rebels, who killed him on the spot.

I had my son aged seven years old with me and the poor boy witnessed everything that happened to me. When the other rebels, who had gang-raped me, saw him, they killed him too – right there in front of my eyes. Then they left me for dead with my new-born child and ran off. It is impossible to describe the agony of watching your own child slaughtered in front of you. I was only able to keep living for my baby's sake but I was not able to do anything for myself for the remaining years of the war. I relied on help from the other villagers who had stayed behind and also survived.

After the end of the war Nyuma Saffa came back to live in the village. This was very hard for me, but what could I do? Then one day some people came from the community-led reconciliation programme, Fambul Tok. They asked whether there was anyone in the village who had suffered a painful experience during the war. I came forward and explained what had happened to me. Then they asked Nyuma Saffa to come forward and explain what had happened.

Finally he came forward and confessed to what he had done. The Fambul Tok committee then asked us to dance as part of a forgiveness ritual. At first I refused. I couldn't bear to hold his hand. But in the end, after much encouragement, I decided that I would dance with Nyuma Saffa. As I took his hand I was sobbing – not out of despair but a sense of relief that perhaps now we could move on from this terrible pain in our past. I didn't expect it, but they succeeded in making peace between us. There is really no problem between us anymore.

www.fambultok.org

Salimata Badji-Knight

Senegal

Circumcising us was their way of seeking revenge – repeating a crime that had been done to them.

Salimata Badji-Knight was brought up in a Muslim community in Senegal, where she was circumcised at the age of five. She moved to Paris when she was nine, and has spent most of her adult life campaigning to prevent the practice of female genital mutilation (FGM) in African cultures. She has also worked closely with the Metropolitan Police in London for their campaign against FGM, as well as many international organizations, including the Women Advancement Forum.

I was five when the women from my village said we were going into the forest. There was a whole group of us girls aged between five and 16; we were happy because we thought we were going for a picnic. But it wasn't a picnic. Even more than the pain and the crying, I remember the shock of realizing that they'd tricked us. I knew they had cut something from me, but I didn't know what. The women were kind in their way, giving us sweets and nice food;

it was their way of asking for forgiveness. But it was also their way of seeking revenge – repeating a crime that had been done to them.

Only later, when I was a teenager, did I realize exactly what had happened. We had been circumcised, supposedly to make us cleaner and to stop us having boyfriends. For my parents, it was like preparing me for marriage – they were doing it for my own good and I accepted this because circumcised Muslim women have stature and respect. Later, when I came to live in Paris, it was a big shock to discover that this was not something that happened to everyone. I was horrified to see Senegalese girls being told they were going on holiday to Africa, when in fact they were being taken back to be circumcised. For my mother, it was a normal part of her culture, and in Paris she secretly had three of my younger sisters circumcised.

I was full of rage and was determined to stop this brutal practice. I started to talk to anyone who would listen about FGM: the social services, doctors, the police and other Africans living in Paris. For a long time I blamed all the women in my community who had united to do this to me, and I blamed all the men for standing by and allowing it to happen. I blamed my mother because she condoned it, and my father because he had never been there to stop it.

When I discovered that most people believe FGM to be a terrible wrong, I felt suicidal. FGM takes away your identity and your dignity. It was only when I became a Buddhist and stopped viewing myself as a victim that I stopped feeling unworthy. Out of rage came compassion, and the realization that this was not my mother's fault, nor the fault of the women who had done this to me. They were simply blinded by tradition.

If I'd held on to all that anger and blame, I'd be dead by now. But my anger has had great results, because it has made me fight to stop this practice.

Today my three sisters work with me to stop the practice of FGM. Even my mother now understands that it's a violation of human rights and has told me that she had never wanted to put me through FGM and had done everything in her power to protect me. Hearing this made me very happy, as it created a closer relationship between the two of us and I no longer blame her for what happened to me.

In addition, before he died, I was able to have a good talk with my father. I opened my heart to him and explained how female circumcision could affect you physically and mentally. He cried and said that no woman had ever explained the suffering to him. Then he apologized and asked for forgiveness. The next day he called my relatives in Senegal and told them to stop the practice. As a result, a meeting was cancelled and 50 girls were saved.

www.womenadvancementforum.com

Robi Damelin

Israel

I saw then that I had a choice about what to do with my pain – to invest it in revenge or try to think creatively.

In March 2002 Robi Damelin's son, David, was shot by a sniper whilst serving in the Israeli army. He was 28 years old. Robi now works for The Parents Circle – Families Forum, a group of bereaved Israeli and Palestinian families supporting reconciliation and peace.

When I was told that David had been killed, the first words that came out of my mouth were 'Do not take revenge in the name of my son.' It was totally instinctive.

David had phoned me just the day before to say, 'I want you to know that I've done everything in my power to protect this road block but I'm like a sitting duck.' Afterwards I had a strange feeling and set about cleaning the house. I'm terrible at housework but that day I worked like a maniac.

David was a student at Tel-Aviv University and he was doing his Masters in Philosophy of Education. When he was called up to the reserves, he came to talk to me. 'What shall I do?' he asked, because he was in such a quandary. The problem is we look at the world as black and white, nobody sees the grey, nobody understands this kid who belonged to the peace movement and who was torn about where his duties lay.

But then he went and I was filled with dread.

He was murdered by a Palestinian sniper who, as a child, had seen his uncle killed very violently. So this man went on a path of revenge and unfortunately David was in the way, along with nine other people.

After David was killed, I was beside myself with grief; friends from all over Israel arrived with food and drink and other little expressions of love. Because I ran a PR office in Tel Aviv at the time, journalists wanted to interview me. In retrospect, I can't believe that I spoke out so strongly so early on – telling the Israelis to get out of the occupied territories.

The Parents Circle noticed what I was doing and its founder, Yitzhak Frankenthal, whose son had been kidnapped and murdered by Hamas in 1994, got in touch. The organization soon became my lifeline. I realized that I shared the same pain as the Palestinian mothers in the group and that with our pain we could become the most effective catalyst for change. I saw then that I had a choice about what to do with my pain – to invest it in revenge or try to think creatively. Since then I have travelled the world spreading the message of reconciliation, tolerance and peace.

A few years ago there came another knock on my door. This time the army told me they had caught the sniper and asked me if I wanted to go to his trial. I said no because what was the point? Would it bring back David if I felt good about the fact that this man was rotting in jail and his mother sitting alone without him? I don't believe in revenge because what revenge could I take to bring David back? But I am also very reluctant to use the word 'forgiving'. Does forgiving mean giving up your right to justice? Does it mean that what they did is OK or that they can do it again? Or do you forget? I simply don't know.

But in the end I decided that I couldn't do this work with the Parents Circle if I wasn't willing to go on a path of reconciliation, and after many sleepless nights I wrote a letter to the family of the sniper which was delivered for me by two Palestinian friends. For a very long time I heard nothing back but then two and a half years later I received a letter through Ma'an – the Palestinian News Service. The Palestinians in my group didn't want me to read it, as it was not exactly a letter written by Martin Luther King.

It was a letter filled with hate and justification for killing, telling me that my son was a murderer. The sniper said he didn't want me anywhere near his family and would not write to me directly. The letter upset me terribly, but the wisest words came from my other son, Eran, who I thought would be so angry. Eran just said: 'Listen, Mum, perhaps this is the beginning of a dialogue.' I also recognized through this process that I was no longer a victim because my life was not contingent on what this man did.

The pain doesn't go away. You could take anything and everything from me, if I could only see David one more time, once more talk to him. I think of him all the time. We were such great friends and had so much in common. At the place where he is buried the parents make beautiful gardens around the graves of their loved ones. I see it as a continuation of motherhood, the enduring need to tend to your child.

www.theparentscircle.org

Assaad Emile Chaftari

Lebanon

I would venture into the jaws of hell if my story could shift just one person's views and move them away from violence.

Assaad Emile Chaftari served as a senior intelligence official in the Christian militia during the Lebanese Civil War (1975–1990) and was responsible for many deaths. In 2000 he wrote a letter of apology to all his victims which was then published in the national Lebanese press. Since then he has dedicated his life to peace building and promoting personal change.

I was educated in a Christian school and studied at a Christian university, and although a few of my fellow students were Muslims, I told myself these were not true Muslims as they were well-mannered and almost Christianized in their ways.

My war against the Muslims began on 13 March 1975 at the start of the Lebanese Civil War. By now friends, teachers and everyone around me would describe Muslims as 'dirty', 'poor', 'lazy'. They would say: 'Look at the ridiculous way they pray...look at all the children they have.' This is how my perception changed. We believed Lebanon had been given by the French to the Christians and that we were the rightful inhabitants while the Muslims were invaders and traitors. We also hated the Palestinians, who by now had made Lebanon their headquarters, gaining support from the Muslim Lebanese in their fight against Israel.

I started off disliking the Muslims and Palestinians, then I hated them, and eventually I was afraid of them and wanted only to destroy them.

When the war began, I joined the telecommunications unit in the Christian forces and later did an artillery course. I was responsible for many deaths whilst shelling the Muslim quarters and it was very easy for me to justify my actions. As our resistance movement grew, I grew with it and eventually became second in command of the Christian intelligence unit. My task was to decide the fate of all those rounded up at checkpoints – whether someone should be spared, exchanged or killed. By now a human being was little more than a product to me. During all this time I still went to Sunday Mass, and if I had anything to confess, I would confess just small mistakes, like losing my temper. I never confessed to killing because I didn't see it as a sin. I was a crusader.

By 1985 the war was getting us nowhere and we decided to negotiate with our enemies. We signed an agreement which in principle put an end to the war. However, 15 days later there was a coup by our fellow Christians. All of a sudden we weren't seen as Christian heroes anymore – but as Christian traitors. The agreement disintegrated, many were killed and I fled from my home with my wife and baby son.

We were thrown into our enemy's mouth and for the following six years we had to live close to the Muslims and Palestinians, protected by the Syrians who were by now our only allies. No one liked the situation and many attempts were made on my life. My wife said she understood the hatred in the eyes of the Palestinians because now she knew what it was like to be despised.

It was in 1988 that my wife attended her very first meeting held by the Initiatives of Change movement. As a good intelligence officer, I asked her what their hidden agenda was, but she had no answer for me and invited me along to their next meeting instead. So I went, but with a gun hidden under my belt and two body-guards waiting outside. At this meeting something began to change in me. It happened when they asked me to look back over my life and all I saw was a path full of blood.

Gradually I discovered I was not the perfect guy I thought I was. I had so much to change on every level. I was still involved in the war but two years later I was invited to my first dialogue meeting. I was told some Muslims would be there and so I'd prepared a very long list of grievances. When my turn came to speak, I took out the list, but as I read it everyone just smiled. Later a Muslim explained he had brought an even longer list. I discovered many things at those meetings. I discovered that Muslims had real names, they had families, dreams and expectations, and that if we did not have the same political opinion we could at least still respect each other.

In the year 2000, when my son was 13, I heard him repeating some very ugly words about Muslims. I was so shocked because this could have been me 40 years earlier. I said to myself, 'Do we really need another civil war for my son's generation to discover that this way of thinking is wrong?' And I realized then that nothing would ever change if people like me, who had discovered the truth, kept it to themselves. And so, some days later, I decided to write an open letter in the press to the Lebanese people, asking for their forgiveness.

Since then I've given my life over to working for peace, even if it means sometimes making great sacrifices. I would venture into the jaws of hell if my story could shift just one person's views and move them away from violence.

www.iofc.org/iofc-international

Linda Biehl and Easy Nofemela

South Africa

I have come to believe passionately in restorative justice.

On 25 August 1993 Amy Biehl, an American Fulbright scholar working in South Africa against apartheid, was beaten and stabbed to death in a black township near Cape Town. In 1998 the four youths convicted of her murder were granted amnesty by the Truth and Reconciliation Commission (TRC) after serving five years of their sentence – a decision that was supported by Amy's parents. Easy Nofemela and Ntobeko Peni, two of the convicted men, now work for the Amy Biehl Foundation Trust in Cape Town, a charity which dedicates its work to putting up barriers against violence. Since Peter Biehl's sudden death in 2002, Linda still regularly returns to Cape Town to carry on her work with the Foundation.

Linda Biehl

When we heard the terrible news about Amy, the whole family was devastated, but at the same time we wanted to understand the circumstances surrounding her death. Soon afterwards we left for Cape Town.

We took our strength in handling the situation directly from Amy. She was intensely involved in South African politics, and even though the violence leading up to free elections had caused her death, we didn't want to say anything negative about South Africa's journey to democracy. Therefore, in 1998, when the four men convicted of her murder applied for amnesty, we did not oppose it. At the amnesty hearing we shook hands with the families of the perpetrators. Peter spoke for both of us when he quoted from an editorial Amy had written for the *Cape Times*: 'The most important vehicle of reconciliation is open and honest dialogue,' he said. 'We are here to reconcile a human life which was taken without an opportunity for dialogue. When we are finished with this process we must move forward with linked arms.'

A year after Easy and Ntobeko were released from prison, an anthropologist who was interviewing them sent us a message to say they'd like to meet with us. They were running a youth club in Guguletu Township where Amy had been killed and wanted to show us their work.

We wanted to meet them. It wasn't about pity or blame, but about understanding. We wanted to know what it would take to make things better. Sometime later we took them out to dinner. We talked about their lives and our lives, but we didn't ask about the past. We were all looking to the future.

I've grown fond of these young men. They're like my own kids. It may sound strange, but I tend to think there's a little bit of Amy's spirit in them. Some people think we are supporting criminals, but the Foundation that we started in her name is all about preventing crime among youth.

I have come to believe passionately in restorative justice. It's what Desmond Tutu calls 'ubuntu': to choose to forgive rather than demand retribution, a belief that 'my humanity is inextricably caught up in yours'.

I can't look at myself as a victim – it diminishes me as a person. And Easy and Ntobeko don't see themselves as killers. They didn't set out to kill Amy Biehl. But Easy has told me that it's one thing to reconcile what happened as a political activist, quite another to reconcile it in your heart.

Easy Nofemela

When the anthropologist suggested bringing the Biehls to meet me, my mind was racing. This was a big challenge. I'd grown up being taught never to trust a white person, and I didn't know what to make of them. Yet I thought that if I could meet them face-to-face, then perhaps they might see that I was sorry. 'Yes, bring them,' I said.

The next day Peter came to Guguletu. I was very nervous, but my first thought was to protect him because there was violence outside. I took him inside my home and told him about the youth club. He was very interested and said Linda would love to see what me and Ntobeko were doing. The next day they came bringing us T-shirts and tickets for Robben Island. I remember Peter was very strong and Linda very shy.

Later we became involved in the Amy Biehl Foundation because they were having trouble in Guguletu where they ran a community baking project. Crime had become so bad in the township that drivers were getting shot at every day. We helped them by talking to the community.

Not until I met Linda and Peter Biehl did I understand that white people are human beings too. I was a member of Azanian People's Liberation Army, the armed wing of the Pan Africanist

Congress. Our slogan was 'one settler, one bullet'. The first time I saw them on TV I hated them. I thought this was the strategy of the whites, to come to South Africa to call for capital punishment. But they didn't even mention wanting to hang us. I was very confused. They seemed to understand that the youth of the townships had carried this crisis – this fight for liberation – on their shoulders.

At first I didn't want to go to the TRC to give my testimony. I thought it was a sell-out, but then I read in the press that Linda and Peter had said that it was not up to them to forgive: it was up to the people in South Africa to learn to forgive each other. I decided to go and tell our story and show remorse. Amnesty wasn't my motivation. I just wanted to ask for forgiveness. I wanted to say in front of Linda and Peter, face-to-face, 'I am sorry, can you forgive me?' I wanted to be free in my mind and body. It must have been so painful for them to lose their daughter, but by coming to South Africa – not to speak of recrimination, but to speak of the pain of our struggle – they gave me back my freedom.

I am not a killer, I have never thought of myself as such, but I will never belong to a political organization again because such organizations dictate your thoughts and actions. I now passionately believe that things will only change through dialogue. People are shocked I work for the Amy Biehl Foundation Trust. I tell them that I work here because Peter and Linda came to South Africa to talk about forgiveness.

Peter was a lovely man. He kept us all happy. It was a great shock when he died. He would say to Ntobeko and me, 'I love you guys. Are you happy, guys?' He tried to avoid things that would upset us. He was like a grandfather to us.

www.amybiehl.org

Khaled al-Berry

Egypt

The most dangerous thing in life is to let people become convinced that truth has just one face.

As a teenager Khaled al-Berry belonged to the radical Egyptian Islamist group, al-Gama'a al-Islamiya. A former BBC journalist, he is now editor-in-chief of dotMSR, a multimedia website. In 2009 Khaled published his book, *Life is More Beautiful than Paradise: A Jihadist's Own Story*.

I was not attracted to the radicals' brand of religion; I was attracted to them as people. I was 14 and the first time I knew one of them, we were playing football and he was a very decent person who took care of people around him. We built up a relationship as human beings. Then we started talking about religion and going to the mosque. This was 1986 and Egyptian society was not religious. We created a new way of looking at life which stated that this life is very short and real life is after death. They taught us that Islam means you can't argue about text because the text is what God said.

Later we were asked to think of other aspects which require you to sacrifice more, like opposing and changing regimes which didn't apply the word of God. We learnt that we couldn't do this except by using violence because God doesn't change our lives and we are tools of God. It was like all revolutionary thinking: you sacrifice yourself for change for the better and for all those poor and unprivileged people.

We were asked to do very small tasks to change the habits of other people. I was asked once to go and follow a tourist who was carrying a bag of wine bottles until we got into a quiet place, then smash the bottles with a stone. Eventually clashes between al-Gama'a al-Islamiya and the regime in Egypt took a bigger shape. I was preaching to people in my school and then my university, and was jailed for six weeks without trial for disturbing the public atmosphere. When friends disappeared, I knew that they had carried out an operation and been killed.

At one stage I thought I would love to be chosen for an operation. The idea of suicide bombing wasn't obvious but the idea of martyrdom was prominent. I would have liked to do something I thought mattered – sacrificing yourself to establish heaven on earth. For me the real question was: 'Am I able to sacrifice more or not?' It wasn't: 'Am I going to do a wrong or right thing?' I knew I was right: the Koran said so. When Islamist people become suicide bombers, they believe that God is ordering them to do it. They are not lying to themselves. They are not bad people but they cannot differentiate between themselves and their ideology.

You only question these beliefs if you find other people and other things to do. For me, the starting point was when I moved from Assiut to Cairo because I thought security services were chasing me. At Cairo University I found people who set up literature meetings and I started thinking as an individual without close monitoring. When you are free in this sense, you come to know exactly what sort of person you are.

I used to think there was only one way to know truth – the divine way, the infallible way. But now I believe that the most dangerous thing in life is to let people become convinced that truth has just one face. At the root of forgiveness and tolerance is the belief that truth has *many* different faces and that the face you see of truth has no greater value than the faces others see.

I don't believe you can have forgiveness without justice, but justice doesn't mean revenge. A lot of people radicalized in the Islamist movement are locked into this primitive thinking that revenge is justice. It's the rationale which says 'The Americans and British killed hundreds and thousands in Iraq and don't even count the bodies, so why blame me if I kill 50 on the tube?' By the same token, Bush sold wars on the idea of revenge.

When I was a victim, I thought protection meant violence. I thought, 'Why should I be tight-handed when others are hitting at me?' I don't believe that now, but equally I feel guilty if I talk in a humanist way about the lives of people who don't have the basic right to live safe in peace. There needs to be transparency before forgiveness.

Kelly Connor

Australia

What I forgive myself for today, I don't know it will apply tomorrow.

In 1971 Kelly Connor, then aged 17, was responsible for the death of a 77-year-old woman in a road accident in Perth, Australia. She has since written a memoir about her experience. *To Cause a Death* is dedicated to both her daughter, Meegan, and Margaret Healey – the woman she killed.

That morning my dad was due to drive me to my job at the telephone exchange but decided at the last minute to have a lie-in, so I drove myself instead. As I climbed a steep hill, I saw a taxi waiting to pull out on the right and – concerned he'd pull out in front of me – I kept my eyes fixed on him. At the brow of the hill I kept my foot firmly on the accelerator but suddenly on the pedestrian crossing in front of me I saw an elderly woman. As I slammed on the brake, she looked up in terror and tried to run – but we collided.

In the silence which followed I could almost have convinced myself it hadn't happened. But, shaking uncontrollably, I managed to get out of the car and drape a blanket over the woman. That's as much as the efficient part of me could manage. Very quickly after that the police and ambulance arrived.

At the police station the officer gently guided me to say I'd been driving at a legal 35mph rather than the 45mph I'd really been doing. It was the policeman's way of protecting me and it was the first time I experienced someone forgiving me. But it took me a long time to see it that way – for many years I wished I'd been imprisoned.

I was informed later that morning that Margaret Healey had died in hospital. At that moment I experienced myself in another dimension of time and space – a sense of total alienation from the rest of the world. That feeling stayed with me for years.

Two weeks later I came home to find Margaret Healey's brother talking to my parents. He told me that he wanted me to know that neither he nor his family blamed me, and nor – he was sure – would Margaret. Deeply generous as I knew this to be, I wasn't in a position to accept his forgiveness. I didn't feel I deserved it. In fact, it just made things worse because I knew I'd given a false statement to the police.

The guilt was so bad that four years later I went back to the police station to confess that I'd lied about the speed I was driving, but the senior police officer I spoke to refused to take my statement. 'Putting you in jail would turn a disaster into a tragedy,' he said.

My family very quickly fractured. The accident happened on my sister's 12th birthday, thus tainting her special day forever. My mother's way of dealing with it was to lay down the edict that we would never talk about it, and my father felt a terrible guilt for not having driven me on that day. Four months later my parents' marriage collapsed and shortly after that my father vanished. We never heard from him again until we were informed of his death ten years later.

For nearly two decades I didn't speak about the accident at all. At one point I was so convinced I didn't have the right to continue living that I tried to commit suicide. I avoided relationships and although I ventured into marriage I left when my daughter was two, taking her with me. But it was the birth of Meegan which made me want to live again.

When Meegan was four, I started on a journey towards self-forgiveness after reading a book about Creative Visualization. I'd tried to imagine how my life would have been without the accident – and during the process I realized that I am who I am because of Margaret Healey. But even allowing myself to consider forgiving myself brought up the full force of guilt again. How can you be grateful for your life when you've killed someone?

Meegan knew nothing of the accident, but when she was 14 I knew I had to tell her; otherwise this secret between us would corrupt our lives. After I told her, she said, in a very matter-of-fact way, 'So this is why we live such a peculiar life.' Her acceptance led me to start dealing with my past.

In 2001 I was asked to write a book about my experience. Going public terrified me but I knew I had to do it to help others who were traumatized by the guilt of causing a death. The book was a great success and the letters started flooding in. The first person to contact me was a woman whose young daughter had been killed as she stepped out on to the road, and her mother wrote, 'Every day for the last ten years I've worried about the driver.'

In that moment I suddenly realized that people have been more forgiving of me than I ever realized. I still almost choke to say I forgive myself and sometimes I can't integrate it into my life, but I've reconciled that that's how it has to be. The moment I've fixed forgiveness, it's no longer real. It has to be changing and constantly challenging. What I forgive myself for today, I don't know it will apply tomorrow.

www.kellyconnor.com

Arno Michaelis

USA

It was the unconditional forgiveness I was given by people who I once claimed to hate that demonstrated the way from there to here.

From the age of 17 Arno Michaelis was deeply involved in the white power movement. He was a founding member of what became the largest racist skinhead organization in the world, a reverend of self-declared Racial Holy War, and lead singer of the race-metal band Centurion, selling over 20,000 CDs to racists round the world. Today he is a speaker, author of *My Life After Hate*, and works with Serve2Unite, an organization that engages young people of all backgrounds as peacemakers.

I grew up in an alcoholic household where emotional violence was the norm and, as a kid who was told I could achieve anything, I reacted to that emotional violence by lashing out and hurting people. I started out as the bully on the school bus, and by the time I was in middle school I was committing serious acts of vandalism.

As a teenager I got into the punk rock scene which for a while was the ultimate outlet for my aggression. But, like any other addiction, my thrill seeking needed constant cranking up, so when I encountered racist skinheads, I knew I'd found something far more effective. I joined up for the kicks and to make people angry.

I was also enamoured with the idea of being a warrior, and, as a skinhead, here at last was my chance to be a warrior for a magnificent cause – to save the white race! I truly believed white people were under threat of genocide at the hands of some shadowy Jewish conspiracy. It made total sense to me, probably because nothing else in my world was making sense.

So I assumed an identity where all that mattered was the colour of my skin. I remember one Thanksgiving dinner, when I was very vehemently and drunkenly spouting off my views, my mother said to me, 'Well, Mr Nazi, did you know that you're one-sixteenth Indian?' That completely shut me up right there and then, but later that night I went back to my own house and continued to drink beer out of glass bottles – until I broke a bottle and slit my wrist with it. That's how convinced I was that my racial identity was all I had.

Once I'd stepped down this path, violence became a self-fulfilling prophecy, so the more violence and hatred I put into the world, the more the world gave it back to me, which of course only further validated all my paranoia and conspiracy theories. I wallowed in violence as a means of self-destruction and stimulation. Using white power ideology as justification and profuse alcohol abuse as a spiritual anaesthetic, I practised violence until it seemed natural, becoming very proficient in aggression. With my bare hands, I beat other human beings to the point of hospitalization over the colour of their skin, their sexuality, or simply just for the adrenaline rush. Kids trying to emulate me did much worse.

I radiated hostility, especially towards anyone with a darker complexion than mine, and I had a swastika tattooed on the middle finger of my right hand. One time I was greeted by a black lady at a McDonald's cash register with a smile as warm and unconditional as the sun. When she noticed the swastika tattoo on my finger, she said: 'You're a better person than that. I know that's not who you are.' Powerless against such compassion, I fled from her steady smile and authentic presence, never to return to that McDonald's again.

It wasn't until I became a single parent aged 24 that I began to distance myself from the movement. I'd lost a number of friends to either prison or a violent death by now, and it started to occur to me that if I didn't change my ways, then street violence would take me from my daughter too. And once I began to distance myself from the constant reinforcement of violence and hatred, suddenly it began to make much less sense to me. At the same time I began to feel I had an identity of my own – and so for the first time I allowed myself to listen to whatever music I wanted to listen to, and watch whatever TV shows I wanted to watch – not just what had been approved by the white power movement.

Soon I got immersed in the rave scene, which couldn't have been more different from the skinhead scene. While there was still a lot of drug use and irresponsible behaviour, there was also a lot of forgiveness. I was embraced and accepted by people who formerly I would have attacked on sight, and that was a very powerful thing for me. But it took me a long time to work through my feelings of guilt and remorse for the harm I'd caused.

I had effectively been on a ten-year bender, but once I quit drinking in 2004, I felt the need to really make a positive impact and speak out publicly against racism and hatred. In 2007 I began writing a reflective memoir and co-founded the online magazine *Life After Hate*. When I was younger, I thought I had created my challenge by declaring war on the world, but I've come to realize that responding to aggression with compassion is much, much more difficult than responding to it with anger and violence.

Forgiveness is a sublime example of humanity that I explore at every opportunity, because it was the unconditional forgiveness I was given by people whom I once claimed to hate that demonstrated for me the way from there to here.

www.mylifeafterhate.com
www.serve2unite.org

Idan Barir

Israel

I don't feel that I have the right to forgive myself and rid myself of guilt or the strong sense of shame I feel.

Idan Barir is a former Israeli soldier in the artillery forces, from Tel Aviv. In recent years he has been an activist with the Israeli–Palestinian movement Combatants for Peace and is currently a PhD candidate in Middle Eastern History at Tel Aviv University.

As a child I had a very clear idea of what patriotism was. I'd grown up with images of the glorious fighting of 1967 and wanted to be like those great Israeli heroes who had entered the old city of Jerusalem.

In 1999, a year after I was conscripted, I was sent to the occupied territories for the first time – to the West Bank, just north of Nablus. It was during the last phases of the Oslo Accords implementation and the region was very quiet. But the next time I was sent to the West Bank my experience was very different. By now the Second Intifada had just broken out and we were sent to a tumultuous area near Jenin. We used an almost deserted settlement called

Kadim, which had just eight families remaining in it, as our base of operations. Descending from this hill-top settlement into the town of Jenin was like going from heaven down into hell.

It was a completely crazy time. Armed with guns, we'd chase boys with stones through tomato and eggplant greenhouses. We were trained to believe that every Palestinian was a threat. By the fifth week, when all the Palestinian greenhouses had been destroyed and trampled underfoot, the military built trenches where tomatoes and eggplants once grew. I remember being very indifferent to the dramatic changes I had viewed in the rural landscape of Jenin during the first weeks of the Intifada. Agricultural scenery was changed in a blink of an eye into giant fields of trenches and tall dirt walls, and I didn't find anything wrong in it. If Palestinians were a threat, we had to do all in our power to thwart this threat.

In April 2000, we were taken to Hebron and posted in a very religious settlement. One of the fiascos of the Israeli operation in that region was Kaleb's Field. The field was owned by Menachem Livni, a settler who was convicted in the early 1980s of leading the terrorist organization known by the name 'The Jewish Underground'. Livni grew grapes in the heart of a small Palestinian town called Bani Na'im. He came to his field every morning at 6am and left at sunset, and ten of us had to guard him and his grapes around the clock. It was during one nightshift here that I became very fearful and began to think what we were doing was ridiculous and redundant. Ten people's lives were being put in danger for the sake of a convicted felon growing grapes.

Once out of the army, I was moved to a reservist unit and in 2006 we were called again to Jenin. Our base was a checkpoint on a very small hill, fenced with high cement walls. We would conduct nightly raids and ambushes, firing tear gas just for the hell of it. For some it was fun, but for me it felt purposeless. Two years later I was sent to Qalqiliya to serve in an agricultural checkpoint. Every morning we'd have a morning briefing on an empty parking lot overlooking Tel Aviv. My commander would point out across the land, trying to make us believe that this was the land we were defending. They needed to give us a purpose. He told us that we would face many threats during our time of duty, including knife attacks and shootings, but the threat to be most afraid of was that of the Machsom Watch – a group of Israeli female peace activists who stand silently by checkpoints in protest against the Israeli occupation. My superior officer said, 'If a Palestinian threatens you, it's very easy because you can shoot them in the head, but unfortunately you can't do that to Machsom Watch activists.'

As it happened, on that very day, the Machsom Watch did come to my checkpoint and I got to speak with one very nice grey-haired woman who reminded me of my grandmother. I didn't accept everything she told me, but I was proud she was there.

A few months later, I was travelling in Germany when I met a Palestinian from Ramallah who was working as a waiter in a coffee shop. His name was Ahmed and he told me a terrible story of how he'd been arrested by the Israeli security forces and held in a secret facility for ten days. The investigator had put him in a coffin half-filled with water and left him there for six days. He said on the first day he believed they wouldn't break him. On the second day he had to shit and pee on himself and his legs began to freeze. On the third day he was shouting and screaming, and by the fourth day he was begging for his life, promising to tell them anything they wanted to know. He was very angry with Israelis and told me that in another time and place he would have killed me. My experience with Ahmed was not easy, even though we had some very pleasant conversations, but it was my first experience of a dialogue with a Palestinian in a non-military setting, one that included serious listening from both of us and that made my rethink many things I used to believe were the truth.

What finally made me realize that violence was not the solution was seeing pictures on television of the Israeli Defence Force (IDF) bombing the outskirts of Gaza with phosphorus artillery shells. In training we had always been told that it was against the Geneva Conventions to use phosphorus, but day after day I watched these bombs being used and then heard the IDF military spokesperson denying it in the evening. I felt my moral world collapsing. I had grown up to believe that the army never lied. This was the start of a new way of thinking for me. I wrote a letter to my commanders and told them I was no longer willing to take part in any fighting in the occupied Palestinian territories.

As an Israeli, I feel so ashamed that our army tells lies. Also, hearing the story of Ahmed made me feel very ashamed of ruthless practices that became all too common and acceptable in Israel. If I had a chance to meet Ahmed again, I would tell him, 'I will fight your war for you, but I want you to convince other people that revenge is not the way forward.'

I'm not looking for forgiveness from those I may have hurt because I know I won't get it. Nor do I feel that I have the right to forgive myself and rid myself of guilt or the strong sense of shame I feel. Forgiveness should be something more practical that both sides can benefit from. If we can tunnel vengeance into something constructive, then this will be the most beautiful interpretation of forgiveness.

www.cfpeace.org

Marian Partington

England

*Forgiveness
began with
murderous rage.*

**In 1973 Marian Partington's younger sister, Lucy, disappeared
from a Gloucester bus stop after visiting a friend. Twenty years
later, the gruesome discoveries at 25 Cromwell Street revealed
that Lucy Partington had been one of the victims of serial
killers Fred and Rosemary West. Fred West committed suicide
before the trial in 1995, while Rosemary West was found guilty
of ten murders and sentenced to life imprisonment. Marian's
memoir *If You Sit Very Still* tells her own story of brutality,
traumatic loss and the restoration of the human spirit.**

As soon as the news came through that Lucy's body had been
found at 25 Cromwell Street, I vowed to try to bring something
positive out of this meaningless trauma.

But first I had to face the truth. Lucy had been abducted,
gagged, raped, tortured and murdered, before she was beheaded
and dismembered. For a year after the finding, her remains were

needed as an exhibit for the defence. I felt an instinctive need to go to the mortuary in Cardiff to hold and wrap her bones. During that moving ceremony something shifted and I made a step towards peace.

In that same year I also began to go on Chan Buddhist retreats. It was at one of these that I made a vow to try to forgive the Wests. It seemed the most liberating, positive way forward. This was uncharted territory for me, but I have always believed there is something good in everyone.

When I came home from the retreat, I had an overwhelming, involuntary and profoundly physical experience of murderous rage: it went…whoosh! All the way up from my belly to my skull. I wanted to scream, pull my hair out, claw at the ground. So, for me, forgiveness began with murderous rage. Until then I hadn't thought of myself as a murderous person, but at that moment I was capable of killing. In other words, I was not separate from the Wests.

At the committal trial, when I saw Rosemary West sitting there, it was almost impossible to match her expressionless face with the endless graphic details of sexual depravities and brutality. But then I heard her voice on tape, shouting, swearing and full of rage, and I began to have some insight into her mind. I later discovered she'd been sexually abused by her brother, then abducted from a bus stop and raped aged 17.

Her story seems to be about the impoverishment of a soul that knew no other way to live than through terrible cruelty. A life deprived of truth, beauty or love. I imagine that the deviant ignorance that fed her sadistic, egotistical crimes was rooted in her ruined, crooked childhood. Will she ever know the sacredness of life? During my time working in Bristol prison on a project about restorative justice, I came to understand that most perpetrators have been victims of abuse in their childhood.

Since then my work has been about connecting with Rosemary West's humanity and refusing to go down the far easier and more predictable path of demonizing her. I take every opportunity to talk about her as a human being.

I once met a mother whose daughter had been murdered. She gave me a phrase that I now have pinned to my door: 'Forgiveness means giving up all hope of a better past.' Gradually, I have grown to face, accept and integrate the unresolved pain of the past. I have imagined something of Rosemary West's suffering, something of Lucy's suffering. I do not wish Rosemary West more pain.

Working towards forgiveness seems to be the most imaginative way of becoming free and offering freedom. It is only something you can line yourself up for; you can't make it happen. But I know it's the only creative way forward, because it allows me to find a positive relationship with my own suffering which can be beneficial to others. In this way I can use my life to transform the cycle of violence. Sometimes I have experienced the sacredness of my own life and the inter-connectedness of all our lives. In this place forgiveness is spontaneous.

Some people have asked whether I feel I'm betraying Lucy by doing this and I say, 'No, absolutely the opposite: I feel I'm honouring Lucy by lining myself up for forgiveness.'

Kemal Pervanic

Bosnia

I didn't decide not to hate because I'm a good person. I decided not to hate because hating would have finished the job they'd started so successfully.

Kemal Pervanic is a survivor of the notorious Omarska concentration camp, which was set up by Bosnian Serb forces in the early days of the Bosnian War. The camp, nominally an 'investigation centre', was uncovered by British journalists in 1992, leading to international outrage and condemnation. Kemal now lives in England, he is the founder of Most Mira charity and is the author of *The Killing Days: My Journey through the Bosnian War*.

I was born in Bosnia in 1968 when ethnicity and religious beliefs didn't matter. Although my mother identified as a Muslim, I had no religion. 'Brotherhood and Unity' was our slogan. After the fall of the Soviet Union, political groups started to form along ethnic lines and I noticed some of my Serbian neighbours looking at me differently. One schoolmate, who I'd always been on good terms with, would no longer greet me because I was a Muslim.

Then, in May 1992, the newly named Bosnian Serb Army began targeting Muslims and my village was attacked. I was captured and taken to Omarska camp where the conditions were terrible; there was very little food, no space to sit, and just two toilets for a thousand people. Luckily, I was with my middle brother and this eased the pain. But we didn't know whether the rest of our family members were alive or dead.

A lot of neighbours used this situation to settle old scores. One of the guards was my former language teacher; another was a former classmate. Many times people were taken out and tortured. Some never returned. When I'm asked now, 'How is it possible for people to turn so suddenly on those they know?' I tell them it takes a long time to prepare people for the slaughter of their neighbours.

I spent the whole time in a state of terror, but I knew I needed to suppress my feelings in order to survive. I became able to watch someone being slaughtered like a pig without crying. It didn't mean I didn't care, but extraordinary circumstances make you react in ways you can't explain.

After ten weeks three British journalists came to Omarska and the world's press got hold of the story. As a result, I was transferred along with 1250 survivors to a camp registered by the International Committee of the Red Cross. The facilities were still terrible but I no longer feared for my life. Finally, we were released on condition that we left Bosnia and signed away everything to the newly formed Serbian authority.

When I first arrived in England, I couldn't talk about what had happened. I felt frozen and didn't trust anyone. It wasn't until I heard that my elder brother and parents were still in Croatia, and were being treated extremely badly, that I finally broke down. In my blackest moments I imagined killing my torturers and feeling absolutely nothing as I did it. Such an act I knew would destroy me.

What saved me during these years was the support I received from some wonderful people.

Ten years later, I decided to return to my village to ask my former neighbours why they'd taken part in the violence. I managed to meet up with two of my former teachers. One of them seemed full of remorse and said he'd never wanted to participate in the Serb National Project, but the other one I didn't believe. He'd been an interrogator in the camps and had clearly enjoyed the job. He wanted me to say that I forgave him, but at that time I couldn't do that because he showed no remorse.

Back in England, I suffered my second breakdown. Returning to my village had been traumatic – my past had been destroyed, the place just grass and rubble. But, despite my trauma, I wasn't filled with hatred. I didn't decide not to hate because I'm a good person. I decided not to hate because hating would have finished the job they'd started so successfully. It would have poisoned me.

Then something strange happened. One cold January morning, I was in the shower when suddenly I found myself saying, 'I forgive you.' Year after year I'd carried the memory of the perpetrators on my shoulders. So when this moment came I felt a huge release. It wasn't a conscious decision to forgive; something just changed inside me. Perhaps it was because my father's recent death had inspired me to make some personal amends (I'd contacted former girlfriends and apologized in case I'd ever hurt them unintentionally). Perhaps I forgave because I realized that death can come at any time and take away the opportunity for reconciliation.

I went back again to Bosnia, and one day during this trip I recognized a former camp guard hitching by the side of the road. I started laughing. My friend couldn't understand why I was laughing, but what else could I do? I didn't want to swear or scream or get violent. I laughed because I remembered the monster this man had been, but now, hitch-hiking alone on a dusty road, he looked almost pitiful. That's what they call the banality of evil.

People describe these people as monsters, born with a genetically inherent mutant gene. But I don't believe that. I believe every human being is capable of killing.

www.mostmiraproject.org

Jean Paul Samputu

Rwanda

The shock was so great that I started drinking and taking drugs to forget. I wanted to take revenge. I wanted to kill Vincent. But I couldn't find him, and so I started killing myself.

Three years prior to the Rwandan genocide, Jean Paul Samputu, at the time a rising star on the East African music scene, spent six months in jail alongside thousands of other Tutsis who had been arrested in their homes. The jails were overflowing, so the government finally released the prisoners, but the situation grew increasingly tense. In April 1994, over a 100-day period, nearly one million Rwandan Tutsis lost their lives at the hands of their fellow Rwandans, the Hutus. Among the dead were several of Jean Paul's family.

When the government started teaching Hutus how to hate, my father warned me to leave the country as I was a well-known Tutsi musician and therefore an obvious target. At first my parents didn't realize that they were also in danger because in the Butare south we lived side by side with our Hutu neighbours and my father would say, 'I trust them, they are my friends.' Even when I begged him to leave, he said, 'I'm 86 years old, I want to die here.'

It took a long time in my village to mobilize the Hutus to kill because some were married to Tutsis. Imagine being told to hate this person you love and who you have been together with for so long.

So I left on foot through the forest and started a music tour in Burundi and Uganda. The news spread abroad quickly that Hutus were killing all Tutsis – that's how I learnt that my parents, three brothers and a sister had been killed.

I returned as soon as the killing had stopped and went straight to my village. The survivors didn't know how my mother or siblings had been killed, but they said, 'Your father was killed by Vincent, your best friend, your father's friend.'

I didn't expect this and when I heard the truth my life changed forever. The fact that it was a close family friend who had done this destroyed me. He was two years younger than me and my closest neighbour, my closest friend.

The shock was so great that I started drinking and taking drugs to forget. I wanted to take revenge. I wanted to kill Vincent. But I couldn't find him, and so I started killing myself. It took nine years for me to deal with my anger, bitterness and desire for revenge. As I moved between Rwanda and Canada, where my wife and disabled daughter lived, anger and bitterness took hold to the point that I could no longer sing or show up on stage. I was an addict, an alcoholic.

All the time some of my friends were praying for me because they knew I was going to die. Then, one day, this miracle happened. In the midst of all this hell, I suddenly felt a strange peace in my heart.

Faith helped me to stop drinking. I had tried many things – drugs, witch doctors, but none of it worked. So I took a Bible and I went to a prayer-mountain, and spent three months away from everyone just to discover God's healing. During this retreat I heard a voice telling me that even if you become a Christian it's not enough; you need to forgive the man who killed your father because you cannot love again if you still have hatred in your heart. And that voice was telling me forgiveness is for you, not for the offender.

Of course, it took time to accept that message, but in the end I had no choice and one day I said, 'YES! I'm ready to forgive.' On that day I suddenly felt totally free. I felt a power that I cannot describe.

Since that time the songs flowed again, thousands of them. And that year in 2003 I won a Kora Award – the most prestigious music award in sub-Saharan Africa. It helped me to go to America with my music where I started to tell everyone about this most unpopular weapon – forgiveness. It's unpopular because it's a hard topic and a difficult process. Some people don't want to teach it to their children, even in the church, because they look in the mirror, and they cannot preach what they cannot do.

By the time I returned from America in 2007. Vincent had been released and I went to my village to speak at the *gacaca* (a traditional court) trial, saying the reason I was there was not to accuse him, but to forgive him and to set myself free. I hadn't known Vincent was actually present until he stepped forward from the crowd and we met for the first time since the genocide. I then told him I forgave him. Telling him this gave me a great peace in my heart. I was a healed man. Afterwards we went to share a meal together and since that time we are often together.

He told me he was surprised that I'd forgiven him. Even though he had repented and asked for forgiveness, he didn't expect my forgiveness. I asked him to tell me where my father was buried. He told me the place and then he explained to me the law of genocide.

The law of genocide is that you must kill your closest friend first, because if you don't then you will be killed. When Vincent told me this, I began to understand how genocide can create a monster from any of us.

www.samputufc.org

Cathy Harrington

USA

*There's so much
we can't explain,
but we need to
be able to love
the questions.*

In 2004 Cathy Harrington's 26-year-old daughter, Leslie, was murdered in a brutal attack in her own home. It was Halloween night when the killer broke in, also taking the life of another of Leslie's housemates. A year later, after an extensive police investigation, Eric Copple admitted to the crimes. Copple is now serving two life sentences with no right to appeal. Cathy is a Unitarian Universalist minister, belonging to a liberal religion that encourages people to seek their own spiritual path. Since her daughter's murder Cathy has devoted herself to campaigning for a fairer judicial system.

When you lose a child, it's like a nuclear bomb has dropped. Your world becomes a barren landscape where nothing grows. It's as if all your landmarks are gone and you don't know where you are anymore. It's taken me a very long time to find my way.

In the summer of 2004 Leslie was happier than I'd ever seen her. Having just graduated, she'd come to live with me near Berkeley, California, where I was finishing seminary college. She got a summer job in the Francis Ford Coppola winery and loved it so much she decided to make a career of it. So when I was called to a church in Michigan, Leslie stayed on in the Napa Valley.

I heard the news from my sister. On 1 November she rang to tell me she'd heard on TV there'd been a murder in a house in Dorset Street where the girls lived. I wouldn't believe it at first but then I rang the Napa police, and when they said, 'We've been waiting for you to call, Mrs Harrington,' my heart just dropped.

It turned out that having handed out candy on Halloween night the girls had gone to bed. But someone had broken into the house and stabbed both Leslie and Adriane. Fortunately, Lauren, whose bedroom was downstairs, was unharmed. The attack on Leslie was so ferocious that the police believed the murderer must have known her.

I was in total shock. What do you do when you hear news like that? Thankfully, Rosemary, who was my advisor in seminary school and a very important person in my life, called and told me to buy an air ticket and fly out to her in California. So I did and Rosemary stayed by my side and protected me during those first terrible weeks.

Leslie had been the outsider. She came from the South, had been a ballet dancer and beauty pageant queen, and the Napa community felt she'd brought this tragedy on them. So, on top of our grief, we had to deal with this as well as the paranoia of not knowing who had killed Leslie. I was distraught and my two sons were beside themselves. It took nearly a year for the police to find the murderer who turned out to be the boyfriend of Adriane's best friend – someone Leslie had never even met. When we found this out, a weight lifted – I'd always known that Leslie was not the target.

The media intrusion was horrible. Murder is entertainment and I realized very quickly that dead people and the bereaved have no rights. The coverage of Leslie's story was sensational, vulgar and diminished her in every way.

At the funeral my boys took me aside and said, 'Don't even think about protesting the death penalty, Mum.' I didn't know what to do because in my heart I didn't want to play a part in anyone else's murder, but I wasn't going to put the life of Leslie's killer above my relationship with my sons. I decided the one person who might be able to help me navigate this process was Sister Helen Prejean who inspired the film *Dead Man Walking* – so I contacted her.

She said it makes sense your sons would want the ultimate punishment for the murder of their sister. But she also told me that when the disciples needed to make meaning out of Jesus' death, they produced the Gospels, and she invited me to write Leslie's gospel. So I started to think about my daughter's legacy. And I immediately thought about how full of love she was and how many friends surrounded her. Sister Helen also talked about the mother of the murderer in *Dead Man Walking* who'd had to leave town because people were so viciously abusing her. When she told me this, it poked a hole in my darkness because for a moment I thought of Eric's mother and realized that there was something worse than being the mother of a murdered child.

During those early years of trying to make sense of such unspeakable horror, I spent a lot of time living among the poor, doing street retreats and visiting the dispossessed in Nicaragua. I found comfort there. If there was a place I could find grace, it was in the streets. The Nicaraguans have a saying that you make your way by walking. And that's what I did – I just put one foot in front of the other.

By the time of the sentencing hearing in 2007, my sons no longer felt they wanted the death penalty. We made it clear to the prosecution that we didn't want to endure a public trial, and if they could work out a plea agreement, then we would prefer it. At first when we went to court there were two sides and I couldn't look at Eric's family across the room, but once we started talking about how we could produce the most compassionate outcome for everyone – whilst still getting justice and protecting society – then the mood shifted.

As the media left the court, Rosemary whispered, 'Cathy, do you want to meet Eric's mother?' I was absolutely terrified but when I saw her coming towards me I knew I needed to. She was trembling – more terrified than me. I was stunned by how similar we looked, and thought, 'Oh my God. I'm her!' Then we just embraced and there was such relief and compassion in that embrace.

After the sentencing hearing we were able to breathe again. We were done. Eric was going to prison and had waived his right to appeal. Now we were left with the task of making meaning and writing Leslie's gospel.

Two years after Leslie died, I read on the news about how the Amish had forgiven the shootings at their school. I said to my grief counsellor, 'Damn the Amish! I don't believe or trust it.' I couldn't forgive, so how could they? My grief counsellor replied, 'Their faith calls them to walk towards forgiveness.' And that's come to make sense to me. It was a decision they made, but I'm not there yet, and the thing that terrifies me most is the thought that one day I may need to meet Eric Copple.

I've been in the dark for many years; it's getting clearer now. Lots of things in life are senseless. There's so much we can't explain, but we need to be able to love the questions.

Hanneke Coates

Indonesia

I thought I had forgiven my Japanese captors, and yet was always aware of the hairs rising in the nape of my neck when I heard a Japanese voice.

Hanneke Coates was born just before the Second World War on the island of Java in the Dutch East Indies (now Indonesia), where her father was a tea planter. After the invasion of Java by the Japanese in 1942, she was forced to spend three and a half years of her childhood in one of more than 300 concentration camps based around the Archipelago. After the war, as was the practice with many colonials, Hanneke's parents remained abroad whilst she and her siblings returned to Holland to be fostered out to a number of Dutch families. Later Hanneke moved to England, where she still lives.

After the invasion all European women and children were advised by the Japanese forces to move to protection camps for their own safety. So we left our homes voluntarily, expecting to be protected, but as soon as the camps were filled, they put barbed wire around us. In the meantime, husbands and fathers were sent to work on the Burma railway line or placed in concentration camps in and around Japan.

We were constantly moved from one camp to another, often transported in boarded-up train carriages without seating, lavatories, food or drink. My final camp was the notorious Tjideng camp (now part of Jakarta) which housed around 11,000 women and children. The camp was one of many set up to intern European civilians, mainly Dutch, as 'Guests of the Emperor' during the period 1942 to 1945. Those of us who ended up there experienced what can only be called 'hell on earth'.

Food was in short supply and we survived on a starvation diet of half a coconut shell with rice and water-lily soup once a day. Water and sanitation were almost non-existent and medical supplies very scarce as all Red Cross parcels were withheld by the Japanese. We all suffered from tropical diseases such as cholera, dysentery and malaria.

The most lasting effect of those three and a half years in captivity was the relentless and total humiliation the Japanese inflicted on us. We were day and night screamed at, publicly disgraced and punished by having our hair hacked off with blunt knives, and regularly lashed with long whips. Many times a day we were herded on to the parade ground to stand for hours in the burning tropical sun and made to bow to our captors. One of my earlier memories is from when I was four years old, when we were made to witness the hanging of two Dutch soldiers. By the end of the war many hundreds of thousands of women and children had died through malnutrition, tropical diseases and lack of medication. I was one of the lucky ones.

In 1948 I was sent to Holland to finish my schooling (11 schools altogether!), living with a number of incredibly cruel foster families. As a planter, my father carried on working first in Indonesia, then Ghana, and since European leave only came round every four years my parents became as good as strangers to me.

Even though the concentration camp years had a deep and damaging effect on us, as a family we simply did not talk about it, as it was a taboo issue back in Holland. The Dutch had endured occupation by the Germans and suffered severe cold winters and hunger too, and therefore they did not want to know about our suffering.

Later, having trained as a nurse, I went to live in England, where at the age of 23 I married an English man and had three children. The traumatic years of my entire childhood had a direct influence on the relationship with my husband, and I allowed myself to be subjected to domestic abuse and years of humiliation.

It was as if the concentration camp years had 'conditioned' me to be humiliated. I had from an early age learned to obey in order to avoid punishment, so when I found myself married to a man who liked to control me, my life continued as the underdog. This dynamic only changed once my children had flown the nest. The fact that I seemed to be enjoying this newfound freedom brought on great tensions and clashes in my marriage. And so, after almost 40 years of marriage, my husband walked out on me, having beaten me up and broken a number of my bones one more time.

It was attending a Christian divorce recovery course at Lee Abbey where I first learned to deal with my traumas through forgiveness. I have never been a hating person, but I learned to acknowledge that forgiveness is a long and slow process. I thought I had forgiven my Japanese captors, and yet was always aware of the hairs rising in the nape of my neck when I heard a Japanese voice.

The Japanese tsunami changed all that. My church asked us to dig deep for the Japanese victims. After a lot of prayer I did just that. It was that one last and final gesture of letting God deal with the residue of my resentment that brought the final healing. I no longer worry about Japanese voices now.

Forgiveness is a healing process and the positive force in my life. It gives me a constant sense of peace and grace. I now share my story in schools, churches and secular groups. Almost always someone will share with me afterwards how my talk has changed something for them.

Forgiveness does not mean that we have to be 'matey' with those whom we have forgiven. I wrote a short letter to my ex-husband saying I was sorry for anything I had contributed to the break-up and that I had forgiven him. I have seen him twice in 13 years. Betrayal is something others do to us, but bitterness is something we do to ourselves. Too often 'unforgiveness' is passed on through generations. If we do not forgive, we lose the joy of living, whereas when we forgive, we release peace and grace and restoration to the forgiven as well as to ourselves.

Mary Johnson and Oshea Israel

USA

It was such a healing poem all about the commonality of pain and it showed me my destiny.

On 12 February 1993 Mary Johnson's only son, 20-year-old Laramiun Byrd, was murdered. The perpetrator was 16-year-old Oshea Israel who received a 25-year sentence for second-degree murder. Many years later Mary visited Oshea in prison and since his release in 2010 they have lived as neighbours in the Northside community of Minneapolis. Mary now dedicates her time to From Death to Life, an organization she founded that uses healing and reconciliation to end violence between families of victims and those who have caused harm.

Mary Johnson

I was at work when a caller rang to ask if my son had come home that night and, if not, I should try to get hold of him. She said she didn't know if it was true but she'd heard that his body was at the morgue. I was so confused and immediately called my sister who called the police department. When she called me back, she said, 'Mary, they said they're coming to see you so it must be true.'

I must have fainted because when I came round my supervisor was holding me. I don't remember leaving the building or taking the short ride downtown, but by the time I arrived at my sister's house they had identified the body.

Three days later I was told they'd picked up the 16-year-old boy who had taken Laramiun's life. I believe hate set in then and there. Here was I, a Christian woman, full of hatred. I was pleased he was going to be tried as an adult for first-degree murder, so when the judge suddenly changed the charge to second-degree murder I was mad. In court I viewed Oshea as an animal and the only thing that kept me going was being able to give my victim impact statement. I was inspired by my faith, and so I ended off by saying I'd forgiven Oshea 'because the Bible tells us to forgive'. When Oshea's mother gave her statement, she asked us to forgive him, and I thought I had.

But I hadn't actually forgiven. The root of bitterness ran deep, anger had set in and I hated everyone. I remained like this for years, driving many people away. But then, one day, I read a poem which talked about two mothers – one mother whose child had been murdered and the other mother whose child was the murderer. It was such a healing poem all about the commonality of pain and it showed me my destiny. Suddenly I had this vision of creating an organization to support not only the mothers of murdered children but also the mothers of children who had taken a life. I knew then that I would never be able to deal with these mothers if I hadn't really forgiven Oshea. So I put in a request to the Department of Corrections to meet him.

Never having been to a prison before, I was so scared when we got there and wanted to turn back. But when Oshea came into the room, I shook hands with him and said, 'I don't know you and you don't know me. You didn't know my son and he didn't know you, so we need to lay down a foundation and get to know one another.' We talked for two hours during which he admitted what he'd done. I could see how sorry he was and at the end of the meeting, for the very first time, I was genuinely able to say that I forgave Oshea. He couldn't believe how I could do this and he asked if he could hug me. When he left the room, I bent over, saying, 'I've just hugged the man who'd murdered my son.' Then, as I got up, I felt something rising from the soles of my feet and leaving me. From that day on I haven't felt any hatred, animosity or anger. It was over.

In March 2010 we gave Oshea a welcome-home party arranged by my organization and some Catholic nuns from the hood; even some ex-gang members from Chicago drove down to witness what was happening. When Oshea told me he wanted to share his story publicly with me so that he could help others, I couldn't believe he wanted to do this. He is my spiritual son. It's not easy for us to stand next to each other, again and again, and share our story, but I say to other mothers that talking and sharing your story is the road to healing.

Oshea Israel

As a child, I never looked at myself in the mirror and thought you're going to grow up a murderer and I'm still trying to figure out how I went so off course to commit such heartache.

That night things got out of hand. I was a 16-year-old at a grown-up's party. There was this whole posturing thing going on. Laramiun was there with his people, I came in with my people and we started playing off our egos. I took it too far.

The court proceedings were a blur. I separated myself – it was just my physical shell going through the motions. For years I didn't even acknowledge what I'd done and would lay the blame on everyone else. I didn't want to hold myself responsible for taking someone's life over something so trivial and stupid. You blame everyone else because you don't want to deal with the pain.

I realize now that as I was growing up I took certain things too personally. If you don't forgive people saying stupid and disrespectful things to you, then you walk around with this resentment, collecting more and more baggage. And if something grows and grows, it's bound to come back to bite you. For instance, I could never forgive how my father's alcoholism meant he was never there for me. I was defined by my disappointment and bitterness. If I'd had more forgiveness in my life, perhaps I wouldn't have exploded at the party that night.

In prison I spent a lot of time in segregation and for a long time had a face on which looked like I didn't care. Then one day I had a sort of epiphany and started to look at how I was living my life. I went through a real growth process. Luckily, I had started changing and educating myself by the time Mary approached me. At first I said no to the meeting because I wasn't ready, but Mary persisted and when she tried again I was in a better place to hold myself accountable. To call myself a man, I had to look this lady in the eye and tell her what I had done. I needed to try to make amends. Whether she forgave me or not was not the point.

I walked in without any expectations and it really put me at ease the way she genuinely wanted to know about me. This was something completely new because when you're in prison no one cares about who you are.

People ask if I've forgiven myself for taking Mary's son's life and I think the process of forgiving myself has started but it's not complete. I also know, however, if I don't forgive myself, I'll walk around feeling guilt and start to self-sabotage. I have to remember I'm a lot different now from that 16-year-old boy who took a life.

Knowing Mary has made me more humble, made me approach things differently and not always expect the worst from a situation. Even at the times I don't believe in myself, when I'm being super stubborn, she's just as stubborn to keep wishing me better, wanting me to make progress. I am more positive now because I have someone in my life who supports and believes in me, even though I know Mary would prefer to be giving all that love and emotion to her son.

I have learnt that if you hold on to pain it grows and grows, but if you forgive you start to starve that pain and it dies. Forgiveness is pretty much saying I give up holding on to that pain. Hurt people usually haven't forgiven and have so much pain they end up causing even greater pain.

www.fromdeathtolife.us

Shad Ali

England

At this point he raised his hands to me in the public gallery, put his hands up against the glass and, with tears rolling down his face, asked for my forgiveness.

Shad Ali, an ex-social worker, is a British Pakistani who has lived and worked in Nottingham all his life. In July 2008 he was attacked when he came to the rescue of two Pakistani women who were being racially abused by a passing pedestrian. Six years later Shad met his attacker at a face-to-face restorative justice meeting.

One warm afternoon in July I was cycling through Nottingham city centre when I heard a man being extremely aggressive towards two Pakistani women who had done nothing to provoke him. I tried to calm him down but this seemed to aggravate him even further, and so, realizing I was not making any progress, I made the fatal error of turning round and getting back on my bike.

The next thing I remember was being punched with such force that I fell to the ground unconscious. Whilst I lay there, the man started stamping and kicking my face repeatedly. I was told later that he had to be pulled off me by members of the public who probably saved my life. By the time I was taken to hospital, I had brain fluid coming out of my nose and was in excruciating pain.

Within four days I'd had major reconstruction surgery – as a result of which the right-hand side of my face is still full of titanium. In the months that followed I had several more operations. I also had emotional and psychological problems. The trauma took a huge chunk out of my life.

When eventually my assailant was arrested, he pleaded not guilty. The first trial lasted a week and remarkably there was a hung jury, but when we went back to court a few weeks later this time the defendant realized the trial wasn't going his way and, knocking on the glass window, he announced he'd decided to change his plea to guilty. At this point he raised his hands to me in the public gallery, put his hands up against the glass and, with tears rolling down his face, asked for my forgiveness.

He received a five-year custodial sentence under an IPP (indeterminate public protection) order. But I felt no sense of satisfaction. I knew from my own life journey that locking away these kind of men without correct input was totally futile.

Forgiveness for me began long before that. It began the day after the attack when I woke up in my hospital bed feeling remarkably at peace, but surrounded by family and friends who were all distraught – particularly my male friends who wanted retribution. But having been on the receiving end of such extreme violence, I couldn't conceive of inflicting similar pain on another human being and made quite sure they knew this wasn't what I wanted. Forgiveness came from wondering how on earth someone could inflict that kind of pain on another human being without feeling anything.

Although my attacker had been using foul, racist language, I didn't believe that his violent actions were racially motivated – he was so full of rage that I think he would have reacted in the same way if I had been white. I couldn't help feeling that he was also a victim of some kind; something had happened in his life which had manifested itself in this horrific, violent outburst.

I received a huge amount of criticism and confusion from friends and family who didn't understand why I wanted to forgive – especially from my wife who initially felt nothing but hatred towards this man. In spite of this, forgiving has really helped me move forward after the attack. It has been about me and has nothing to do with the man who attacked me. And yet, from the beginning, I wanted more than anything to meet my attacker.

After years of persisting with my request to meet him, I was finally allowed to exchange letters with him, and I found out that he was full of remorse and wanted to meet me, too. It took many months of preparation but finally a day was fixed for our meeting at the prison where my attacker was serving out his sentence.

I tried not to have any expectations of what that day would bring. Once we shook hands, we spontaneously hugged, which was totally unexpected, and I became very emotional and started crying. During the restorative justice meeting we shared our individual experiences from the day of the attack and also a bit of our life stories. By the end of the meeting, it felt like we had become friends.

Restorative justice introduced an element of humanity into a situation which had dehumanized both the attacker and myself. The process may seem difficult, but I think victims and offenders can get so much out of it. The only way to resolve conflicts between people is to sit together, talk, and find a way to move forward.

Riham Musa

Palestine

Even though I was a little girl, I felt more powerful than the soldiers because I was the person with right on my side.

Riham Musa is a lawyer living in Tulkarm in the West Bank. At the age of 15, she was shot in the stomach by an Israeli soldier as she approached a checkpoint armed with a kitchen knife.

One day, when I was 15, I started chatting to a group of friends about the occupation and about suicide bombings. We all agreed with suicide bombings as a means of resistance, but none of the others would ever have done it. However, I told my friends that I was thinking of becoming a suicide bomber. I was feeling desperate. The life we were living, the economic situation, our education – it was all terrible; we would often be prevented from getting to school for days at a time. All around me I saw young people getting killed. Our whole lives were ruled by the Intifada. It was a culture of violence and there was no escaping it. We tried to find something else to talk about, but there wasn't anything.

How can girls get together in Tulkarm and talk about make-up and fashion?

It was a Thursday, the day when we always visited the family graves, and so I went to visit my father's grave for what I thought would be the last time. The discussion about suicide bombings had stayed in my mind all day, and when I got home I took the only weapon available to me – a kitchen knife – and went down to the checkpoint without telling anyone. I had a feeling that I was superwoman, that I could kill all the soldiers at the checkpoint without doing any harm to myself. Even though I was a little girl, I felt more powerful than the soldiers because I was the person with right on my side.

But when I actually got to the checkpoint, I was suddenly very afraid. I couldn't go through with it and just stood there frozen to the spot. The soldiers saw me standing there, staring at them. They thought I was a suicide bomber and started screaming at me. Then they started shooting. One of the bullets hit me in the stomach and I collapsed. I lay on the ground for four and a half hours as they checked for bombs. Once they realized there were no bombs on or around me, I was taken to the nearest hospital before being sent to prison. After ten months I was released on health grounds, and because I was young and hadn't actually threatened anyone with the knife.

I was worried about going back to school because it's not acceptable for women to be involved in violent action. But in the end it wasn't so bad, and in fact I started doing better in school than before. I felt as though studying was my way out of this misery, and I chose to study law as a more effective way of defending the Palestinian people.

I believe violence breeds violence and there's no choice now for me other than to find another way. When I decided to use violence by taking the knife to the checkpoint, even though I didn't use it,

I brought violence upon myself. I now want to use the law and not weapons to fight the enemy. This feels like the right path.

I still hate the Israeli army but I don't feel violent towards them anymore. I'm a forgiving person and it's not in my nature to hate people, but because of the way we live in the West Bank, hatred has been forced upon me. There's no point engaging with the military because for them non-violence can never work, but with ordinary Israeli citizens I'll use non-violence as a way forward. The citizens of each country have gone through much suffering, and this suffering unites us.

It's not easy to talk of forgiveness in the midst of violent conflict, and forgiveness is not just mine to give. There are many repercussions, and it is not for me to forgive my mother's tears.

www.combatantsforpeace.org

Bjørn Magnus Jacobsen Ihler

Norway

The core issue when dealing with violent extremism is recognizing that we all dehumanize each other.

Bjørn Magnus Jacobsen Ihler is a survivor of the July 2011 attacks on Utøya island in Norway, where right-wing extremist Anders Behring Breivik shot and killed 69 people and injured 110 others. Most of the dead were students attending a summer camp organized by the AUF, the youth division of the ruling Norwegian Labour Party. Breivik had earlier that day carried out a bomb attack on government buildings in Oslo, killing eight people and injuring 209. He was charged with both attacks and in 2012 received a 21-year prison sentence for voluntary homicide. Bjørn is now working against extremism and hatred through a variety of means, including writing, talks, film-making and theatre productions on related topics.

In the afternoon of 22 July we were all gathered in the main meeting room, where we were told there had been an explosion in Oslo. Some people looked up the news on their smartphones. The pictures of our hometown looked like downtown Bagdad so it was pretty obvious this had to be a bomb. We were advised to remain on the island as it was presumed to be much safer than returning to Oslo.

As we gathered in the campsite we heard this popping noise that sounded like firecrackers. Then I saw this man coming over the hill and a few people ran towards him. The next thing I knew he was shooting at them. I was pretty sure this had to be someone kidding with us but I couldn't gamble on it so I ran into the woods with one of my friends. In the woods I noticed this eight-year-old boy who was the son of one of the security guards on the island. He was clearly in shock and I figured we had to help him and so we found a hiding spot. There were about 600 people on this tiny island battling for a few hiding places.

It felt like forever, lying there trying to keep this kid calm. Then I saw a group of people running through the woods towards us. In that crowd was another child – the son of the other security guard. The boy and I joined the crowd and ran along with the second child. By now there were about 30 of us running pretty fast. It struck me then how extremely quiet such a large group can be; we were so soft on our feet.

But then, as we ran along, we came across a most terrible sight – a pile of dead bodies blocking the track. In the midst of the bodies a cell phone was ringing. I realized this must be someone worried sick trying to reach a loved one. Someone who would never get a reply.

We ran to the southern tip of the island, from where we could see a helicopter in the sky and across the water the longest line of blue flashing lights I'd ever seen. We all felt relieved. I gave the kids my phone and had them call their mothers, who were not on the island, telling them that to call their fathers might potentially reveal their hiding spots. Then I called my own father to tell him I was safe.

At that moment, an armed policeman came out of the woods from behind us, saying the bad guy had been caught and we were all safe now. But then he raised his gun, pointed it towards us and started shooting. I jumped in the water and the kids followed me. I swam straight out, but sank due to wearing a heavy woollen jumper. As I stood up in the water to pull it off, I looked back towards the island and saw Breivik take aim at me. I was absolutely certain I would die. It was an extraordinary moment that is hard to describe. I felt this peace inside me but also this overwhelming emptiness; it was a feeling of my soul leaving my body.

Thankfully, Breivik missed and I threw myself back into the water – water now red with the blood of my friends. In order to get out of Breivik's aim I swam for my life around the corner of the island, eventually hiding in some bushes. The boys still following me.

After what seemed like an eternity, a man wearing a police uniform came out of the woods. We thought it was Breivik again, but this man put his gun behind his back and was able to convince us he was a real policeman and that we were finally safe.

During the next hour we managed to get on a boat back to the mainland. It was chaos there too, with a massive row of ambulances and people everywhere. We stood for a while with blankets round us and then a bus picked us up and drove us to the nearest hotel, where the boys were reunited with their mothers. I found out later that both their fathers had been among the first to be killed. It was chaos at the hotel too as parents started turning up. Thinking back, I found that part even worse than the island, knowing that a lot of parents would be returning without their children.

Around midnight my parents arrived with some dry clothes and we drove back to Oslo. The next few days were very difficult and surreal as I tried to come to terms with what had happened. My anxiety levels were high and I felt completely numb; I'd jump at every noise and every sight of the police. I saw a psychiatrist, who offered me pills, but the only thing that helped was talking to other survivors. Later I reached out to the Norwegian Centre for Violence and Traumatic Stress Studies, where I received intensive care.

For the next week or so the Oslo Delegation of the Labour Youth Party held various meetings, during which lists of the dead started coming out. Reading the lists was always extraordinarily upsetting as I recognized the names of friends while also realizing some names represented great individuals who I'd never have the honour of getting to know.

It helped that I was studying in England at the time, and just two months later I returned to Liverpool. It gave me a distance from it all, a chance to get back into some sort of routine. In some ways this was the best way of dealing with the trauma.

That autumn there was a hearing about the further imprisonment of Breivik. I persuaded my lawyer to let me go to court. I wanted to see Breivik again. Meeting him in court was a very important moment for me because I realized he could no longer point a gun at me. I saw him then as just another human being with no power to hurt me anymore. This was a significant step in the process of rebuilding my life, and in understanding that the core issue when dealing with violent extremism is recognizing that we all dehumanize each other.

I believe that we have to recognize Breivik's humanity. I find people's efforts to dehumanize him really scary because that's what he tried to do to us. At times people have refused to say his name, which makes him almost half godly. It reminds me of the *Harry Potter* novels, where the name Lord Voldemort is so feared: a name should never have that kind of power. Norwegians try to dehumanize Breivik by calling him a monster or evil, and leading up to the trial there was public pressure to perceive him as insane; to encourage people to believe that Utøya was caused by one single madman, almost like a natural disaster. It was as if they were trying to write it off. But there's a great danger in doing that, as we need to recognize that these things may happen again.

I don't know if Breivik is capable of remorse and I don't honestly care. People find it odd that I consider him so unimportant but I prefer to try to stop people harming others now than to think about what Breivik did in the past. I was given the gift of life and if I can spend my time making sure that one single person doesn't have to go through what my friends and I went through then this work will be worth it.

Forgiveness is perceived differently in Norway than in the rest of the world, and is often misunderstood here. When Desmond Tutu suggested that Norway needed to forgive it caused massive outrage. This frustrated me because I'm sure Desmond Tutu didn't mean forgive in the sense of excuse, or give someone a free pass to repeat the offence. I think his views are closer to mine, about accepting and being able to move on while still recognizing the pain. This type of forgiveness is about finding some wisdom that we can take out of what has happened to ensure violence doesn't repeat itself.

www.againstviolentextremism.org

Marina Cantacuzino's background is in journalism. Her work has appeared in most mainstream publications in the UK, including *The Guardian, The Telegraph, The Independent, The Times, The Observer*, plus many magazines both home and abroad, and most recently in a regular blog for *The Huffington Post*. She has collaborated with NGOs on overseas campaign stories and in 2001 co-created the One in Four exhibition as part of the Department of Health's Mind out for Mental Health campaign. In 2003, in response to escalating global conflict, Marina embarked on a very personal project collecting stories in words and pictures from people who had lived through violence, tragedy or injustice and sought forgiveness or reconciliation rather than retaliation or revenge. From this, along with photographer Brian Moody, she created 'The F Word' exhibition: a collection of images and personal narratives from around the world exploring forgiveness and understanding in the face of atrocity. The success of the exhibition, which launched in London in 2004, led to Marina founding The Forgiveness Project. Marina is married and lives in London.

The Forgiveness Project

The Forgiveness Project is a UK-based charity that creates opportunities for people to consider the limits and possibilities of forgiveness. It works with individual personal narratives to examine how concepts of forgiveness, reconciliation and conflict resolution can be used positively to break the cycle of harm and violence. At the heart of the organization is 'The F Word' exhibition, which has been seen by 70,000 people worldwide. The charity has also developed an award-winning prison programme, RESTORE, which adopts restorative approaches and narrative learning techniques to tackle offender behaviour. The Forgiveness Project is a secular organization working with people of all faiths and none.

All royalties from the sale of this book will go to The Forgiveness Project.

www.theforgivenessproject.com

Photo Credits

Eva Kor | Grant Stapleton

Ray Minniecon | Charlotte Sawyer

Jayne Stewart | Uncredited

Bud Welch | Brian Moody

John Carter | Katalin Karolyi

Ginn Fourie and Letlapa Mphahlele | Louise Gubb

Bassam Aramin | Dubi Roman

Madeleine Black | Leila Black

Sammy Rangel | Mark Seliger

Anne Marie Hagan | Randy Dawe Photography

Camilla Carr and Jon James | Brian Moody

Jo Berry and Patrick Magee | Brian Moody

Magdalene Makola | Brian Moody

Samantha Lawler | Louisa Hext

Martin Snodden | Brian Moody

Katy Hutchison and Ryan Aldridge | Brian Moody

Gill Hicks | Brian Moody

TJ Leyden | Mark Seliger

Idan Barir | Dubi Roman

Geoff Thomson | Steve Ullathorne

Grace Idowu | Brian Moody

Jude Whyte | Katalin Karolyi

Wilma Derksen | Marina Cantacuzino

Satta Jo | Kalilu Totangi

Salimata Badgi-Knight | Brian Moody

Robi Damelin | Brian Moody

Assaad Emile Chaftari | Jo Berry

Linda Biehl and Easy Nofemela | Brian Moody

Khaled al-Berry | Brian Moody

Kelly Connor | Brian Moody

Arno Michaelis | Jeff Pearcy

Marian Partington | Brian Moody

Kemal Pervanic | Brian Moody

Jean Paul Samputu | Brian Moody

Cathy Harrington | Marina Cantacuzino

Hanneke Coates | Brian Moody

Mary Johnson and Oshea Israel | Louisa Hext

Shad Ali | Brian Moody

Riham Musa | Dubi Roman

Bjørn Magnus Jacobsen Ihler | Zara Drummond

'Resentment and bitterness are cancers of the soul. Forgiveness is a healing balm. It is costly but effective, as this book so clearly demonstrates.' | TERRY WAITE CBE, humanitarian and author

'Confronting, inspiring and unforgettable. The stories in this book not only show the challenges and complexity of forgiveness but reveal unexpected pathways to creating a more tolerant and empathic world, and why we should consign revenge to the dustbin of history.' | ROMAN KRZNARIC, author of *Empathy: A Handbook for Revolution* and founding faculty member of The School of Life, London

'These testimonies show the power of forgiveness as a force for renewal and redemption that can harness reconciliation to positively transform the lives of victims and perpetrators.' | PETER TATCHELL, political campaigner

'There are many, many stories (and fine photographs) in this book, and dipping into them on a grey, cold, rainy day was like walking into a room where all the lights blazed and a fire welcomed. I felt immeasurably better. Proud to be human. Hopeful that, despite all the evil that is perpetrated by the lost, ignorant and wicked, enough good people are spreading the messages which cancel it out. Uplifted, because it is true that "to err is human, to forgive divine". And if this is the finest aspect of the human spirit, then one thing is sure: there are many saintly souls walking the face of the world, teaching the rest of us how to be better.' | BEL MOONEY, journalist and broadcaster

'This book, in which the depths of human sadness are related alongside astonishing accounts of hope, courage and beauty, gives the lie to much that is said and written about forgiveness today. The introductory essay, and the stories that follow, point to the extraordinary range of experiences and situations where forgiveness is somehow relevant, and where it sometimes, often unaccountably, heals and transforms even the most wounded and broken. This is challenging and mysterious stuff, and it will draw a deep and different response from all who open themselves to the pain, truth and transcendence documented here.' | STEPHEN CHERRY, Dean, King's College, Cambridge University and author of *Healing Agony: Re-Imagining Forgiveness*

'This reassuring and uplifting book testifies to the truth of forgiveness – freestanding, not dependent upon faith, but upon humanity. It is both provocative and full of hope.' | JON SNOW, journalist and presenter

'The testimonials in this book have taught me a great deal about forgiveness, which I think I thought was something rather easier than it is. They make me weep and they make me really think about what it is to forgive and what it is to try to understand someone instead of demonizing them. I think this is probably one of the most important projects in the world today.' | EMMA THOMPSON, actor

'I have seen, in warzones across the world, how destructive our human desire for revenge can be. It leads to perpetual conflict and inflicting our own sense of loss and grief on countless others. Marina Cantacuzino's work, in this important book and beyond, is a reminder that there is an antidote. These tales of forgiveness are the balm that can soothe our all too angry world.' | DAN SNOW, historian and TV presenter

'Marina Cantacuzino's new book asks us to consider the most challenging question: Is it possible for a victim to forgive the perpetrator? Presenting us with heart-breaking and astonishing examples, she shows the answer is "yes" – even when the victim is a grieving parent and the perpetrator is the murderer of that parent's child. Forgiveness allows the victim to recognize the humanity of the perpetrator (who may himself be a victim), to re-humanize him. And forgiveness is the antidote to a life imprisoned by bitterness and hatred. This book is an invaluable contribution to the debate surrounding peace and reconciliation.' | PROFESSOR SIMON BARON-COHEN, Cambridge University